How Would You
Play This?

How Would You Play This?

How to Think Your Way to Winning at Pool

GEORGE FELS

CB
CONTEMPORARY BOOKS

Library of Congress Cataloging-in-Publication Data

Fels, George.
     How would you play this? : winning techniques for mastering
pool setups and shots / George Fels.
       p.   cm.
    ISBN 0-8092-2956-0
    1. Pool (Game).   I. Title.
   GV893.F46   1998
   794.7'3—dc21   97-44707
                                         CIP

Interior design and production by Hespenheide Design
Cover design by Todd Petersen
Cover photograph © Chris Cheadle/Tony Stone Images
Back cover photograph © Artville, LLC.

Published by Contemporary Books
A division of NTC/Contemporary Publishing Group, Inc.
4255 West Touhy Avenue, Lincolnwood (Chicago), Illinois 60646-1975 U.S.A.
Copyright © 1998 by George Fels
Printed in the United States of America
International Standard Book Number: 0-8092-2956-0
 18   17   16   15   14   13   12   11   10   9   8   7   6   5   4   3   2   1

For Dale, Adam, and Sam Fels,
who among them solved all my problems

CONTENTS

How Would You Play This?

INTRODUCTION

If you have sufficient hand–eye coordination for any sport that is played with a ball—in fact, any other sport at all—then you can most likely be taught how to pocket balls on a pool table. After all, no particular strength is required for pool, nor is it even desirable, and a pool stroke is one of the simplest physical moves man has ever figured out for himself; ideally, nothing moves except one forearm and the eyeballs. So with a good teacher and a few hours of dedicated practice, you can start making shots with some consistency within a matter of days.

Note, however, that I didn't say that you could be taught how to play pool.

That's a bigger difference than you might think. The vast majority of recreational players simply try to shoot balls into holes, and while that's unquestionably great fun and the soul of the game, it's not really pool playing, any more than shooting hoops is playing basketball. The true game of pool is fantastically complex and mostly mental, not physical; some experts consider the ratio to be as high as 80:20. Your logical first step in making the transition from pool shooter to pool player is simply to recognize that such a difference exists.

After that it's largely a matter of how well you learn (as with any other endeavor, no two students will progress at exactly the same rate), and especially how strong your aptitude is for something called spatial relations. Your spatial skills were probably tested at some point during high school. On paper, it has to do with identifying identical shapes in different attitudes; on the pool table, it has to do with recognizing position *patterns*, meaning which ball goes with which to create the most efficient sequence.

That's what this book is designed to test, bring out, and develop in you. As with my previous books, the instruction is at a reasonably advanced level. I'm assuming that you already have some shotmaking ability; after all, you must be able to sink the ball you select, and it would be even better if you had some comfort with using various areas of the cue ball. Each of the book's three sections presents feasible playing situations from pool's major games, and asks you to identify the correct next shot. By all means, strive for your own answer—*with a reason or reasons for it*—before you glance at my solution. (If we disagree, by the way, and you still think your reasons are just as good as mine, there's nothing that says mine are chiseled in stone. The more important point by far is to have good reasons for your shot selection. Do not simply take the shot that looks easiest or the one you saw first.)

For each diagram, you'll be given not only my solution and reason(s), but a playing principle that you can take forward and utilize in your own game without waiting for the identical table layout to come up again. While any number of good players can spot the right shot virtually at once, you'd be surprised at how many would have trouble telling you *why* it's the right shot. That's not coincidence; it's because when good players hit their stride, their right brains kick in and they cease to rely on words at all, playing instead on instinct and feelings. (It's what athletes in other sports call "the zone"; pool players refer to it as "dead stroke.") You'll get there, too, but before you reach that level, you need a problem-solving foundation.

Let's get you one.

STRAIGHT POOL

Even though it's less likely than it used to be that you play this game, Straight Pool remains pool's all-time great teacher. No other form of the game allows you (at least theoretically) to shoot any ball on the table into any pocket at any point in the game. Straight-Pool position-playing options are therefore rich indeed. If you can learn to think your way correctly through Straight Pool, your Eight-Ball game should improve virtually at once, and it will help your Nine-Ball playing more than you might think. To that end, here's a good playing tip: no matter what your pool game of choice, your warm-up should include at least 30 minutes of Straight Pool.

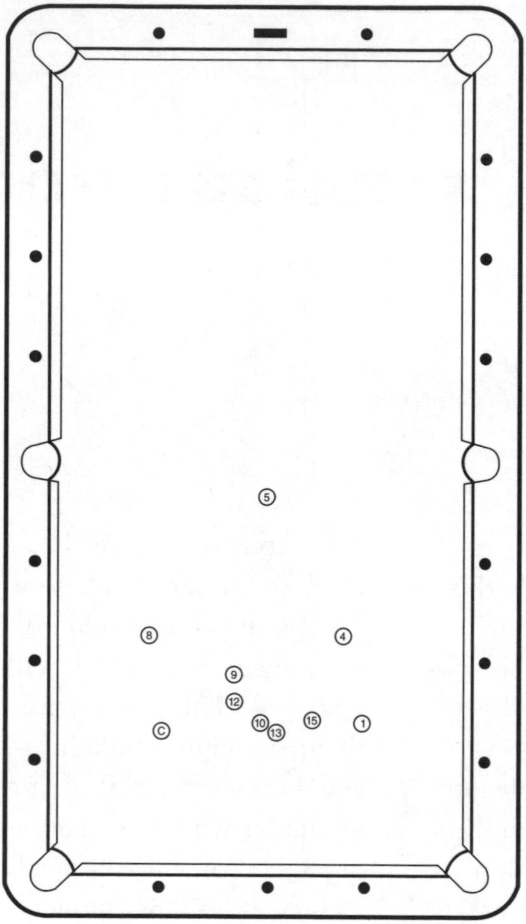

Diagram 1. That 10-13 combination can't miss.

Yes, the 10-13 is "dead," and it's yours just for sending your cue ball in between the 12 and the 9 at decent speed. But why do that, when by shooting the easy 9 in the side and killing the cue ball, you've got the 15, then the 12, then the rest while hardly disturbing a second ball?

Point to remember: *Don't put more balls in flight simultaneously than you have to.*

Diagram 2.

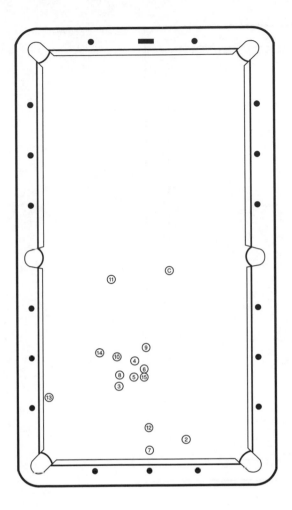

Here's a good example of the virtue of patience. Many players, especially if they've just broken the balls and are getting their momentum going, would drill that 10-ball as a secondary break shot. But there's so little angle to it that you can't separate the cluster very well without overhitting. With all those other open shots, starting with the 11, you'll have plenty of chances to play better shape on the 10, or even use another ball.

Point to remember: *Don't speed up and get rambunctious just because things are going well; think first.* This is an extremely common flaw among intermediate players.

Diagram 3.

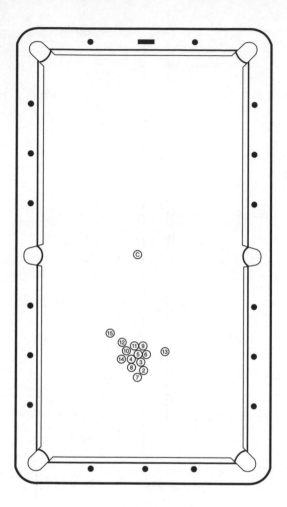

Looks like a win-win situation, but actually the 13 is a much wiser choice, because it lets you draw the cue ball back toward you while those clustered balls are moving in the opposite direction. In order to shoot the 15 at this angle, you'll have to follow into the cluster, in the same direction the broken balls are moving, and it's too easy to get trapped in there.

Point to remember: *Plan your break shots as thoroughly as you can.*

Diagram 4.

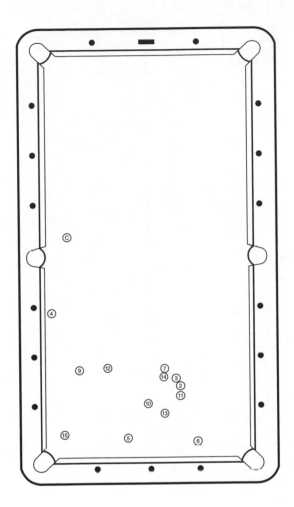

The 4 is a tempting target—the closest object ball almost always is—but that 4-and-9 tandem looks even better if you can save them for last. Play the 15-ball instead, but try to *maximize* the shot by using left-hand draw and spinning the cue ball to where you can make either the 5 or the 13 in the same pocket. If you don't get to use the 13 to separate the clustered balls, you can still use the 6 to get to the 12.

Point to remember: *Look beyond the obvious . . . and stay alert for cue-ball locations that offer you multiple shots.*

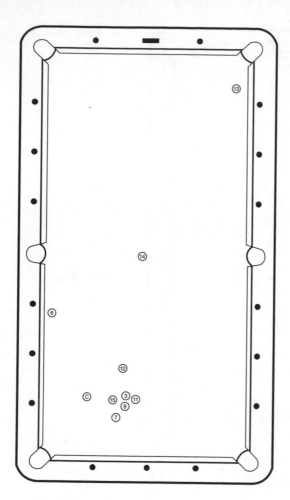

Diagram 5.

Don't shoot the easy 7-ball; it doesn't do anything to help you solve the problem of that four-ball cluster. Shoot the 12 in the side, drawing back a bit to where that slightly off-angle 15-8 combination shot is easy and helps you separate the 11 and the 3.

Point to remember 1: *Deal with problems sooner rather than later.*

Point to remember 2: *Look beyond the obvious.*

Diagram 6.

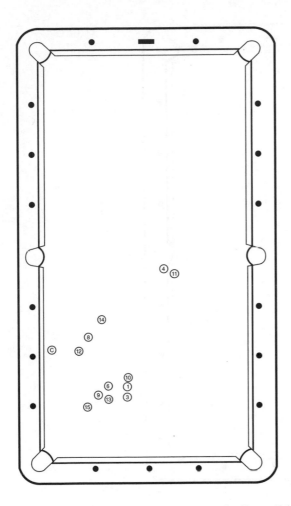

You've got a couple of options here. You could use the 8-ball now to deal with the 11-4 problem early, and then knock off the cluster later with the 12. I'd prefer to save the 12 for the next rack, and instead use the can't-miss 9-13 to separate the cluster now. (Position for the 8 and the 14 into the nearest side pocket should be easy once I deal with the unclustered balls.) It's also worth noting exactly *how* the balls will be broken: the cue ball is going to have to come off that 9-ball to push the 6 into the 1- and 10-balls; the 9 figures to sit there like a lox even after it's struck, and might even be my next shot.

Point to remember: *Make your break shots as precise as you can—and again, deal with problems as early as feasible.* It's like life.

Diagram 7.

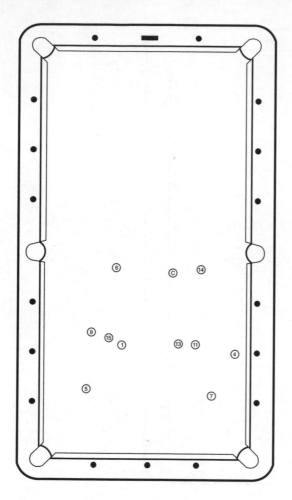

Easy side-pocket shots look inviting—but, whenever possible, you should really be thinking about saving one for your *last* shot of the rack, not necessarily your next one. Side-pocket shots gen-erally help you optimize your position for any break ball near the top or side of the rack. There are a couple of points to be learned here.

Point to remember 1: *Don't be too eager to shoot balls now that you may need later.*

Point to remember 2: *Always clear paths to the corner pockets early.* In this case, it's key for you to get the 5 and the 7 out of there so the 15-, 1-, 13-, and 11- balls all become potential break shots for your next rack. If you want to use the 6 now, make sure your next shots after that are the 9 and the 5; if you use the 14, then continue to the 4 and the 7. But whichever side-pocket shot you choose, leave the other for last.

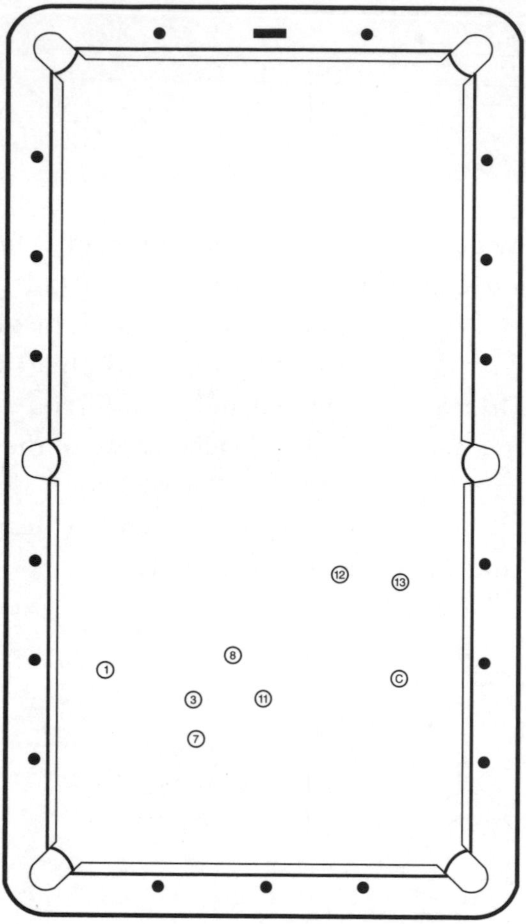

Diagram 8. There's room to make the 7-ball.

But so what? Most players do look for corner-pocket shots first—but in this case, shooting the 7 will most likely move your only real break shot, the 3, out of there. So go around the perimeter: 13-12-1-7-11 (in the side) and 8 (in the opposite side), leaving the 3 for the next rack.

Point to remember: *Always watch for these circle-the-pattern opportunities*, and again, don't move balls unnecessarily.

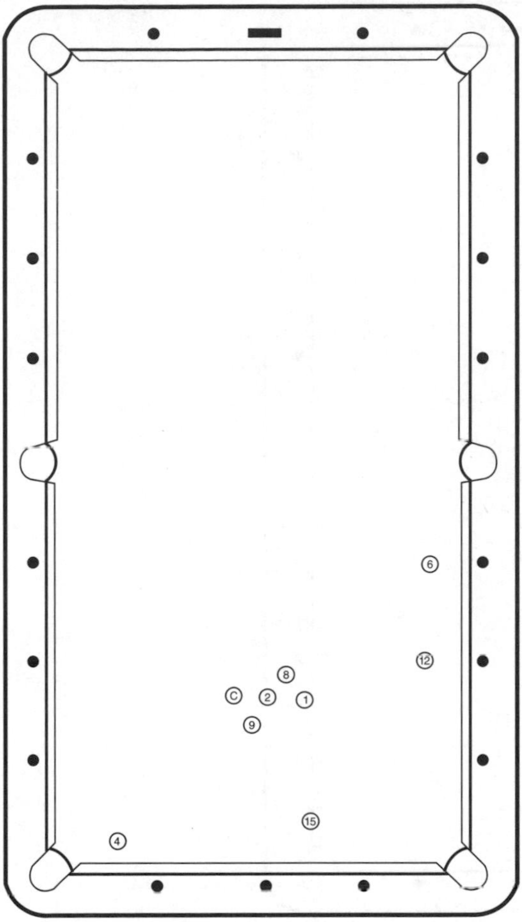

Diagram 9. It's easy to get to the 15 after the 4.

Easy but wrong; you'll probably move the 12 and/or the 6 when you pocket the 15, and you want to save those two. The correct next shot is the 2 into the corner pocket opposite where the 4 is now. That lets you *put the cue ball somewhere with multiple options*: the 8 in the side, the 9 in the corner, or the 15. So hit the 4 with enough follow to bring your cue ball in an area nearly parallel to the third diamond, but well off the rail. Also, as opposed to Diagram 8 where you were shown the value of picking balls off the perimeter of the pattern, here's a way of *cutting across the pattern diagonally*. Both opportunities come up all the time.

Diagram 10.

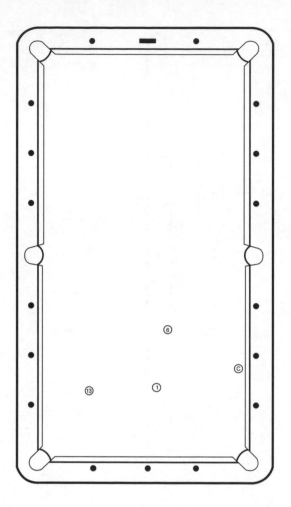

Even though we've already examined the virtue of saving a side-pocket shot for last whenever possible, you needn't be enslaved by that. Obviously you're going to save the 13 here; if you shoot the 1 now, at the angle shown, how can you be certain of advantageous position on the 6? By playing the 6 straight into the side now and following to where you can cut the 1 into the opposite corner, you create a two-rail cue-ball route around the 13 that delivers reliable break-shot position. This option, too, comes up with striking frequency.

Diagram 11.

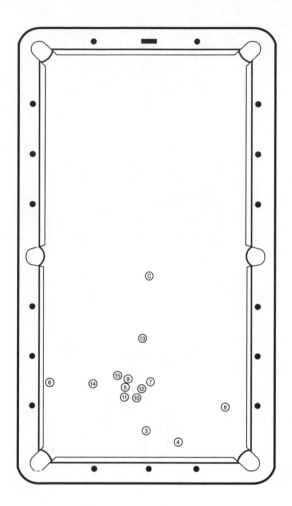

Either the 15 or the 14 is a good shot with which to rebreak the cluster. But clear out the 8, 3, and 4 first, because (a) you don't have an ideal angle on either the 15 or 14 yet, and (b) even more important, you want that area where the 3, 4, and 8 are clear because that's the direction you'll be breaking the balls in.

While you generally want to rebreak clustered balls as soon as possible, you must also be prepared to delay that until all systems are go.

Point to remember: *Think as far ahead as you can without making yourself bonkers.*

Diagram 12.

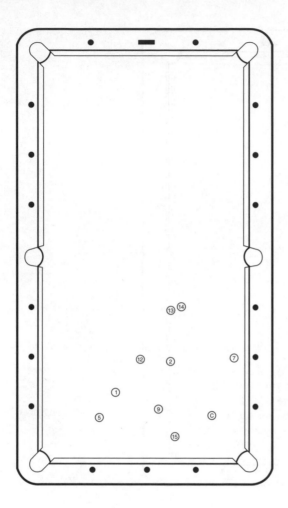

Ninety-five percent of all players would play the ball immediately in front of them, the 15. But note what an excellent chance the 5 gives you to get to center table, from where you can pick off either the 13 or the 14 and set up an easy pattern that leaves either the 7 and the 13 or the 7 and the 14 for last to create break-shot shape on the 2.

Point to remember: *Look at all four corners of your layout for logical sequences.*

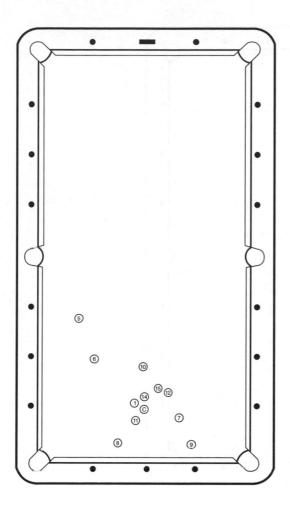

Diagram 13.

What's important here is not the shot so much as the correct progression: 7-10-14, all in the corner pockets. Note that you make the 14 pocketable by sinking the 7 first, an extremely important Straight Pool principle that we've already pointed out: always clear out paths to the corner pockets for other balls to follow, because the bottom two pockets are where 90 percent or more of good Straight Pool is played. Everything sort of unlocks once the 14 is gone. It's another example of cutting across the pattern diagonally, or, as I call it, cutting across midtown.

Diagram 14.

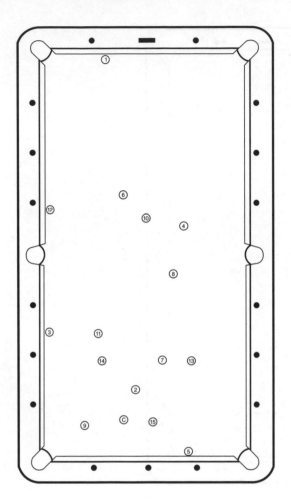

You could be forgiven here for choosing the easiest shot of all, the 9-ball. Just to be sure to play it correctly, which means playing position for the 1 next. Using right-hand English (3 o'clock on the cue ball), use the track between the 14 and the 3, then between the 6 and the 10. (You could also use the 5 to accom-

plish this. But the 15 wouldn't be a wise choice, because you're too likely to run into the 13 and move it unnecessarily.) The only real risk is in getting too close to the rail where the 1 sits.

Point to remember: *Always try to pick off balls on the perimeter of your pattern early.*

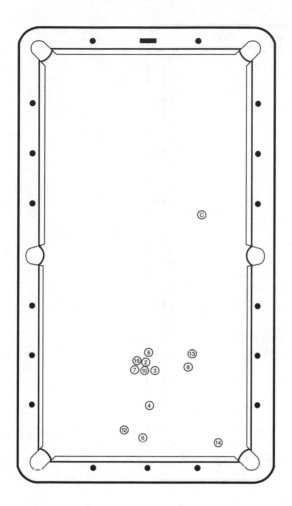

Diagram 15.

The temptation here is to use the 14 as a break shot right now, and while that might work, a better option is to use the 14 to go between the 4 and the 12, hopefully obtaining an angle where you can use the 4 to begin chipping away at that cluster. If you can do that, you'll have two safety-valve shots, the 12 and 6, for insurance when breaking with the 4. There are two concepts worth remembering here.

Point to remember 1: *The insurance shots just mentioned are an invaluable ally when rebreaking the balls*, so strive for plans that include them.

Point to remember 2: *Don't be too eager to use "hangers" for break shots.* They're tougher than you think.

Diagram 16.

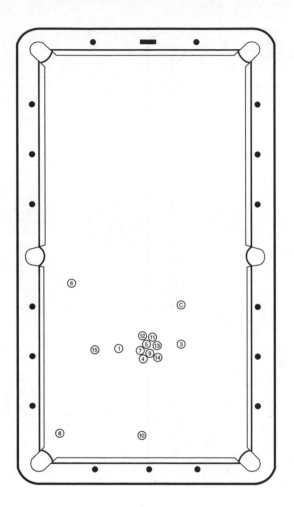

You've just broken the balls quite well, with an immediate chance to break the rest with the 3. But think a bit further than that. You'll be breaking balls in the direction of balls that are already loose, creating uncertain position and possible further clusters. So use the 6 to get to the 8; play the 8 either softly for the 10, or spin under the 10 (with low left English) to get back to center table for either the 1, 15, or 3.

Point to remember: *Think about the consequences of your secondary break shots.*

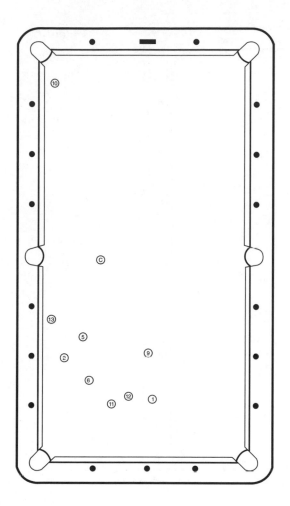

Diagram 17.

Normally it would make sense to get the 10-ball out of the way early. But here, why count on drawing the cue ball half the length of the table (since there isn't much angle on the 10 now)? Play the 13 first with right-hand draw, so you can get a more advantageous angle on the 10 to come back down the table more easily.

Point to remember: *Make things easy on yourself as often as you can.*

Diagram 18.

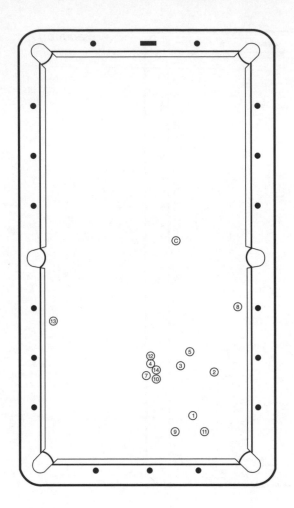

(For the **very** advanced.) You could use the 3 to open the clustered balls right now—but what can you be sure of next? The 1-11 combination shot will be no picnic if the broken balls themselves don't yield anything. Much smarter to shoot the 2 with follow, and try to just pass the 1. Then you can use the 1 to separate the cluster, secure that you'll have the 9 or 11 next no matter

what. (You'll also be saving the 3 as a potential break shot for the next rack.) Again, *arrange sequences that include safety-valve shots whenever possible,* and *try to avoid break shots in which you depend on shooting one of the broken balls next.* That combination of playing concepts will have you playing for certainties instead of probabilities, exactly where you want to be.

Diagram 19.

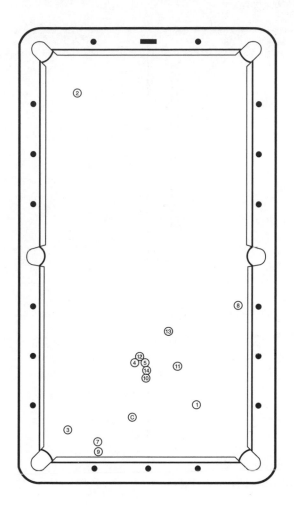

Clearly you've got to go up-table and get that 2, and you could easily use the 3 for that (with right-hand draw and some speed). But if you do that, what will you play for after the 2? The 1? Maybe, but position is too uncertain with the 11 and the 13 sitting in front of it like that; even if you clear those interfering balls, you might have an angle that requires you to run into the 7- and 9-balls unnecessarily. Instead, use the 7 (with *left*-hand draw) to get on the 2 (going two rails around the 1), saving the 3 for next no matter where your shot on the 2 takes your cue ball.

Point to remember: *If you're going to go up and down the table, save yourself easier shots.*

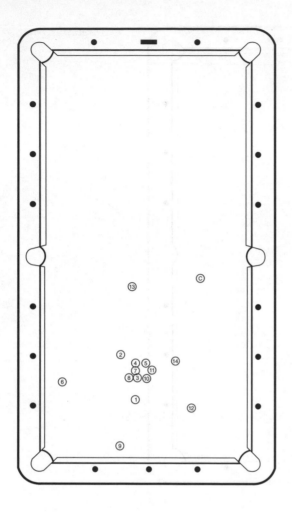

Diagram 20.

Not a bad leave at all, from a typical break shot; open shots are available, including at least two (the 2 and the 14) that can help you separate the still-clustered balls. So let's play position for them correctly, and select a shot that lets us play shape with the most certainty. If you shoot the 12 from here, you'll probably run into the 9 (no good); the 13 may carry you into either the 6 or the 2 (also no good). So make it that unobvious 2-ball where you won't move anything else unnecessarily, and proceed from there.

Diagram 21.

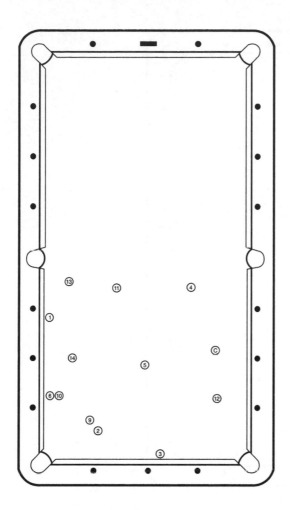

There are many open shots here; the point to recognize is that even with this smorgasbord to choose from, a modest problem still exists. The 6 and the 10 still block the path of the 1 and the 14, and there's only limited space to play position for them. So go after them now, popping in the 9 with a smart center-ball hit. Correctly struck, your cue ball should drift off at a 90-degree angle, right in between the 1 and the 6.

Point to remember: *Get balls off the side rails early in your sequence.*

Diagram 22.

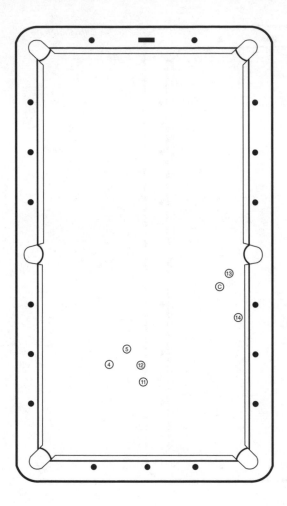

Don't you dare shoot that cinch in the side. Use the 14 to get at the 12; from there you can deal with the 5, the last problem ball facing you (into either the side or a far corner). Because of its extreme ease, the 13 should be left for last, saving the 4 for the next rack. Again, make balls on or near a rail an early priority in your sequence, not a late one.

Diagram 23.

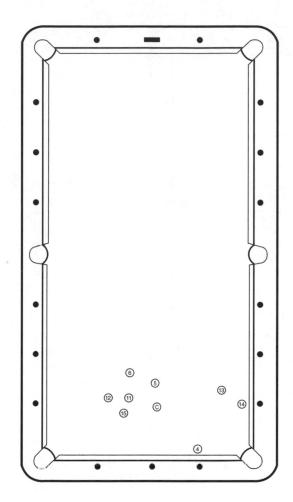

Either the 15-ball or the 4-ball seems obvious here, and with the balls this open, you could probably negotiate this layout somehow by beginning that way. What I want you to start looking for are opportunities like the 6 in the side, which lets you come cleanly back in for all those cinches. Learn to *inspect your layout from all sides*, not just from behind the cue ball.

Diagram 24.

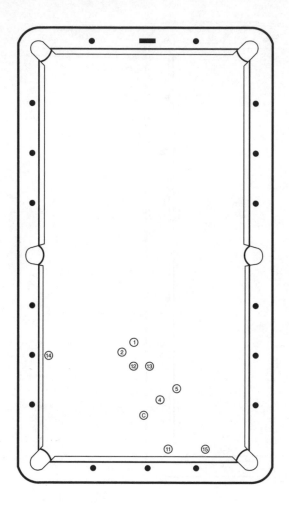

Of course, play the 15—but *don't* play for the 11 next. (This is an extremely common position error.) Leave the 11 there and play shape for the 12- or 13-ball next, so you can play the 1 in the side or far corner and leave the 2 in the clear as a break-shot

option for the next rack. A simple example of three principles at once: look beyond the obvious, look for approaches that take you diagonally across your lay-out, and *leave one ball on the bottom rail until you've solved all your other problems.*

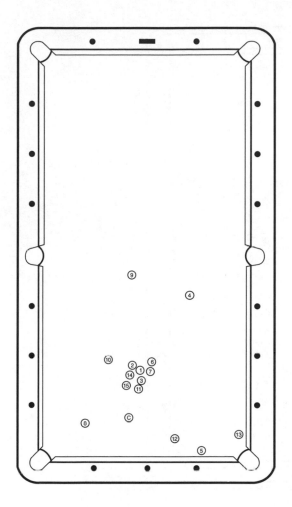

Diagram 25.

This time, the obvious shot—the 8-ball—is correct. What's important is that you see the potential patterns shaping up already. Use the 8 for position on either the 9 or the 4. From there you have your choice of separating the clustered balls either with the 10 or with the 12 (which you get to by playing the 13, and by now you recognize that this option also creates a safety-valve shot, the 5-ball). You really should be able to run this entire rack. Again, learn to examine your layout from all angles.

Diagram 26.

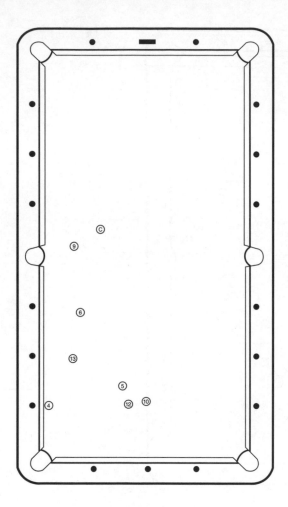

Play the 9—but correctly, by drawing back for the 5 next. If you shoot the 4 immediately after the 9, your position is too uncertain. Leave it there; it can help you get to the 6 for last, saving the 13. By shooting the 5 after the 9, you either separate the 10- and 12-balls or play them in cleanly. I know we've already

looked at the advisability of taking balls off the side rail early whenever possible; it's possible, but not especially feasible here.

Point to remember: *The game will demand that you occasionally break every single position rule of thumb you learn.*

Diagram 27.

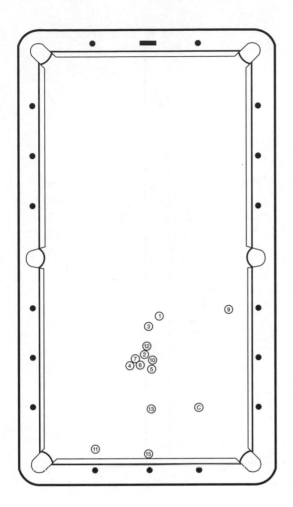

Even though you now have ideal position on the 13, it'd be worthwhile to shoot the 11 with draw first and try to regain the same position. *One ball is all you ever want on that bottom rail.* If you don't get quite back to where you want on the 13, you'll still have the 3-, 1-, and 9-balls available to continue your run.

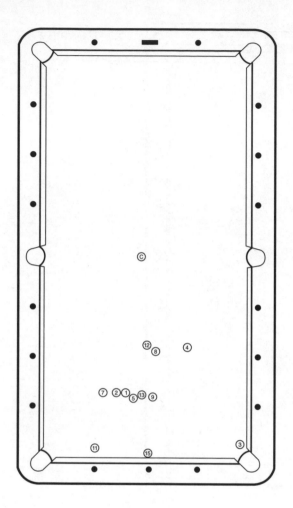

Diagram 28.

Go ahead and play the 7. The thing to note is the nature of that cluster; your impact on the 2 could move every ball in the line, and that's what you should strive for. Use center ball and good speed. Even if you don't get a shot out of the broken balls—

unlikely, given where the 3 is— you can still count on the 12 or 8 in the side.

Point to remember: *When opening up clusters, try to chart the flight of as many balls as you can.*

How Would You Play This?

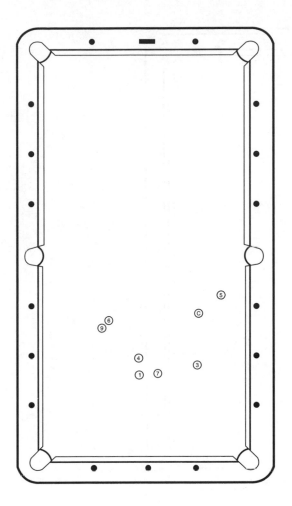

Diagram 29.

You've got shots here, but nothing you can save to get you into the next rack. This is what's called manufacturing a break shot: play the 1 with draw and bump the 7 a few inches, to a good break-shot location. You'll still have the 3, 5, or 6 for next. Sometimes there *is* purpose in moving a second object ball.

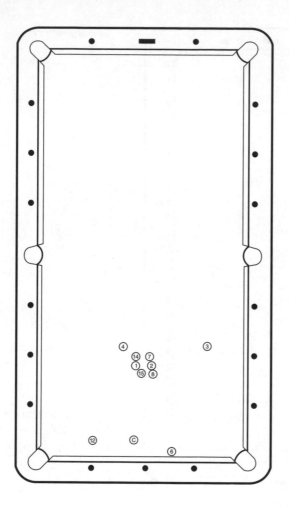

Diagram 30.

As obvious as it seems to play the 12 and the 6 in either order, either would be wrong. Best would be to use the 12 to get position on the 4 in the same corner, saving the 6 as a safety valve until all the clustered balls have an open path to a pocket. A weaker plan would be to use the 6 to try and get break-shot shape on the 3.

Point to remember: *One ball on the bottom rail is too good a friend to take off early.*

Diagram 31.

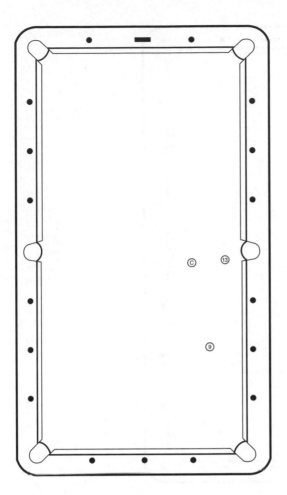

Looks pretty good, doesn't it? But don't settle for a stop-shot that leaves the cue ball next to where the 13 is now. Use soft reverse follow (high left-hand English as diagrammed) and cheat the side pocket slightly. You'll improve your break-shot angle, by getting your cue ball closer to the 9-ball.

Point to remember: *Always try to maximize your position when you can do so without jeopardizing your shot.*

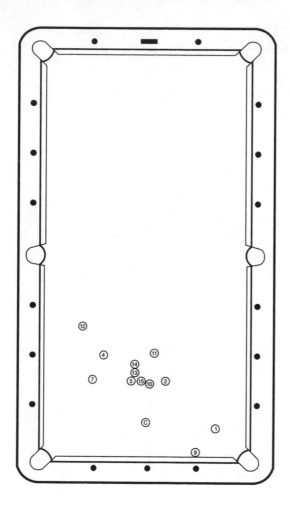

Diagram 32.

Using the 9 as a break shot, with the 1 for your safety valve, *might* work, but I believe a better plan would be to shoot the 1, holding it up with reverse (right-hand) English, for position on the 11 in the side. You'll be traveling toward center table on your break, and that's ideal. If you're not comfortable with side-pocket break shots (you should be), use the 1, with high left, to get on the 12 in the opposite corner.

Point to remember: *Break shots from the rear, especially off rail balls like the 9, carry inherent risks.*

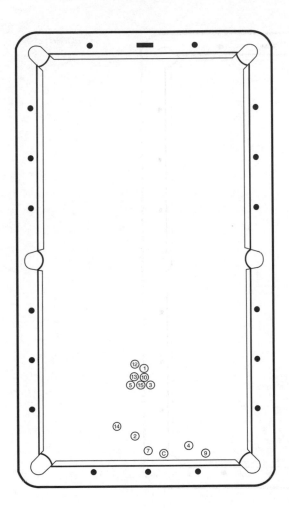

Diagram 33.

Many players, having just broken the balls, would impulsively try to rebreak with the 7. But take a hike around the table (a super idea any time the balls have been broken), and you'll see it's much wiser to take the 9 softly with a tad of reverse (high right), playing for break position on the 2. You get a better break shot and a safety-valve shot (the 4) as well.

Point to remember: *Don't let your momentum cost you good shot-selection decisions.*

Diagram 34.

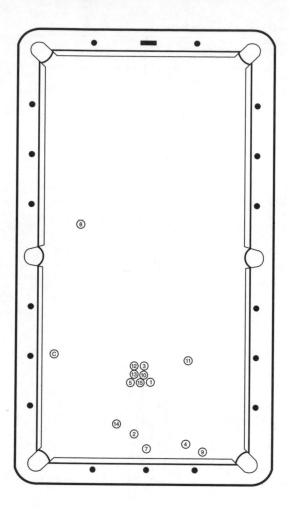

Clearly you have to use the 8-ball, into the near corner pocket, for position on the 11. But instead of using right-hand draw on the shot, use left-hand follow. Your draw position, if it doesn't "bite" off that opposite side rail, could leave you too long. Follow position moves you toward your next shot, not away from it, even though it's a three-rail cue-ball route instead of a one-rail one. But hitting the ball that thin, you should be able to get back close to center table, even with medium English.

Diagram 35.

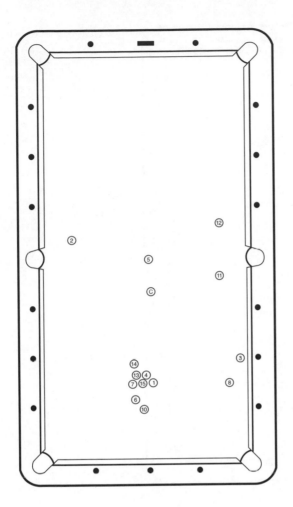

As good as the 3-8 sequence looks for breaking the cluster—especially with the 11 right in front of you to get to it—a better plan would be one that includes the 2-, 5-, and 12-balls; they're of no use. So go 11-12-2-5 to get you to the 3. And if you don't

have ideal break position on the 8—which is sitting a little low for my tastes anyway—use the 8 to get on the 10 and/or 6.

Point to remember: *Take off useless balls early.*

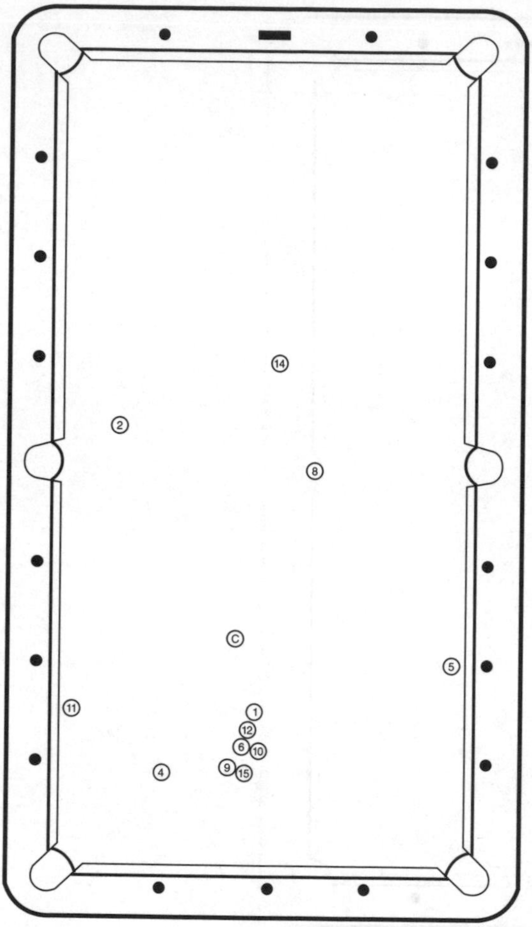

Diagram 36. The 9-15 combination is "dead."

The concept here is identical to the last one: the dead 9-15 will let you open the cluster, and the 4 gets you to it ideally—but don't do that. Instead, use your modest angle on the 4 to try for decent shots on the worthless 8 and 14, and maybe even the 5. You can always get position on the 9-15 off the 11.

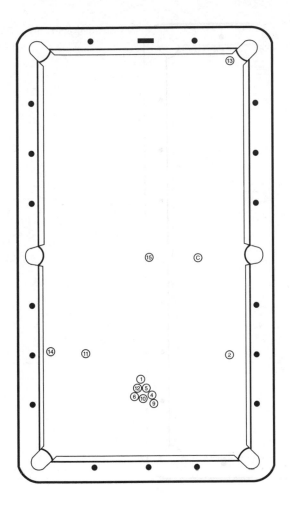

Diagram 37.

Yes, the cinch 15 should come off early—but in this case, second. Take the 2-ball first, and draw back reasonably for the 15. The reason you save the 15 for now is to help you get optimal position on the 11 for the break; the reasons you take the 2 now are (a) because it does you no good and (b) because you'll be breaking the balls in that direction, and want the rail clear.

Diagram 38.

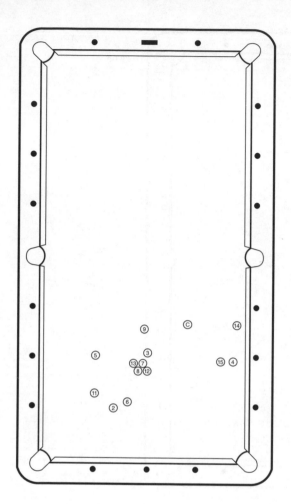

The 15-ball is your easiest shot, but the 4 is a better one. Why? Because it lets you more easily get your cue ball back to center table, from where the 9-, 3-, 5-, and even 11-balls (leading to the 2 and the 6, if you need them to rebreak) are available. If you play the 15 now, there's too much risk of grazing the 4 and/or the 14, making your position uncertain.

Point to remember: *Certainties are way better than probabilities.*

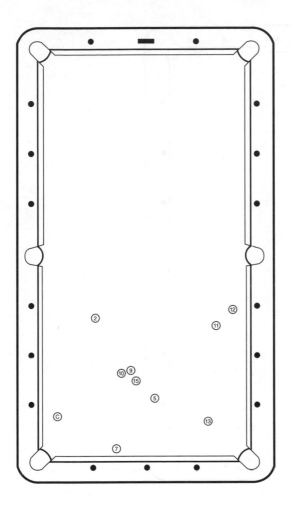

Diagram 39.

Bet you're getting the idea by now: the 13 is obvious, but the best shot is the 7 with left follow. You're trying to go between the 5 and the 13, for an angle on the 15 where you can nudge the 9- and 10-balls apart. You then have two potential break shots into the next rack (the 9 and the 10), a key shot to get to them (the 2), and even a safety valve when you shoot the 15 (the 5). Now *that's* pattern play!

Diagram 40.

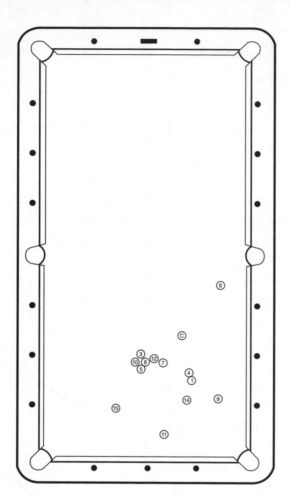

The 6 seems obvious here, and you could proceed that way. But since you're obviously going to have to rebreak from the rear, that 6 could be a valuable ally for break-shot position later in the rack. Play the 9 with soft follow instead, and rebreak with the 11. It's good to save easy side-pocket shots for later, and especially for last, in the rack.

EIGHT-BALL

Welcome to the world's most popular pool game by far. It's correctly played utilizing Straight-Pool principles, with several important exceptions: no more than 8 of the 15 balls are yours to shoot legally, and Eight-Ball will frequently confront you with situations where the correct shot selection involves pocketing *no* balls. (*Important:* In assessing those diagrams captioned "The balls have just been broken," remember that under current rules, neither player is committed to either striped balls or solid ones until someone legally sinks a ball *as intended*; that player then plays the remainder of those balls for the game. In other words, balls that happen to fall on the break stay down, and the breaker continues his turn at the table, but he is still allowed to shoot at anything he wishes.) Eight-Ball is well worth a book of its own, but for now, understand that most of the time, it's counterproductive to pocket your striped (or solid) balls unless those shots lead you directly to an outright win. So the problems in this section involve not only questions as to which ball to shoot, but whether to shoot any at all. The balls in these diagrams have been deliberately left "unstriped" with the intent of helping you *focus*; that is precisely what you need to do to win at pool.

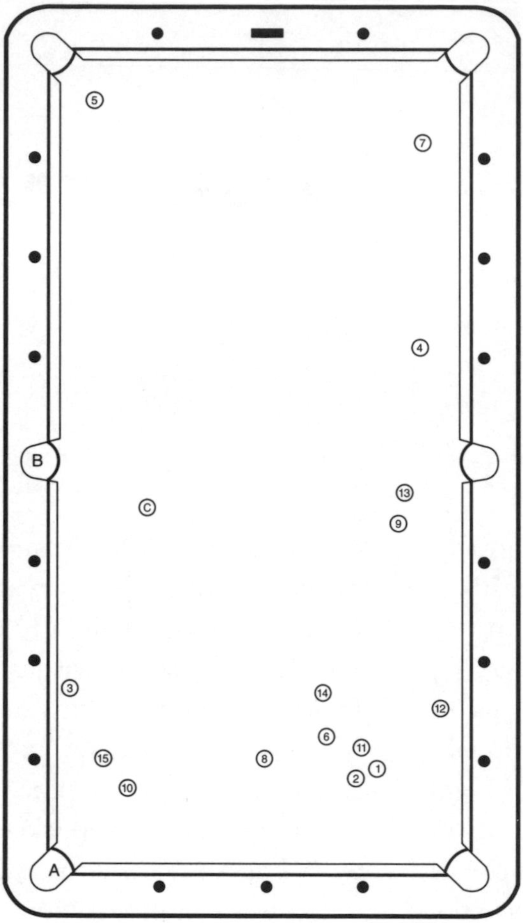

Diagram 41. The balls have just been broken.

With the balls this wide open, a competent player could run out the game choosing either stripes or solids. But note that the stripes can be run just as they lie with no trouble; because the 1 and the 2 are in tight quarters, solids could give you a problem, especially if your cue ball runs into the 11 when sinking the 1 and/or the 2. Choose stripes and go 13, 9, 12, 11 in pocket A, 14 in side pocket B, 15, 10, and 8 in the opposite side.

How Would You Play This?

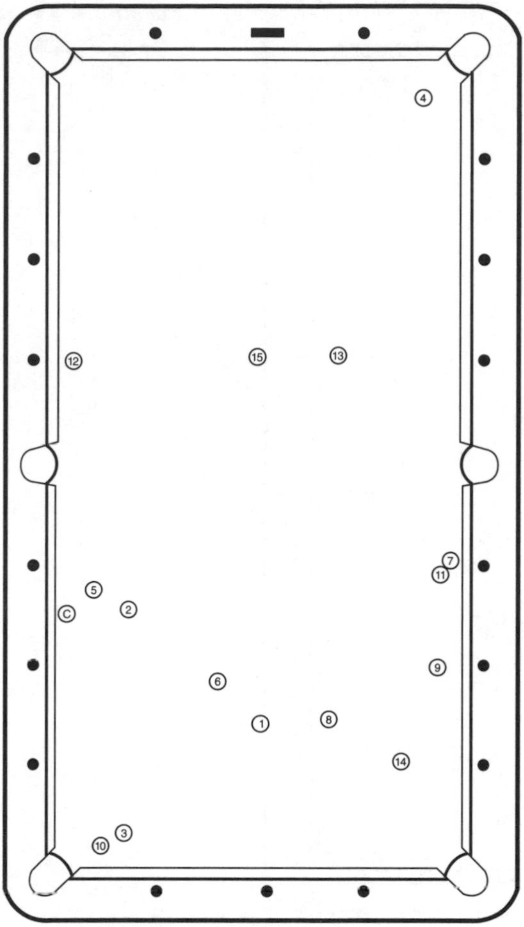

Diagram 42. The balls have just been broken.

Stripes look tempting here—but if you choose them, how are you legally going to sink your 10-ball, with your opponent's 3-ball right in front of it, and what are you going to do to free up that 11? Sink the 1 so you can commit to solids, then use your 3 to sink your opponent's 10 and leave the cue ball on the bottom rail, with the 3 capturing that pocket for you. Let the other guy try to solve the remaining problems. Once he moves his 11-ball, even if accidentally, you should be home free.

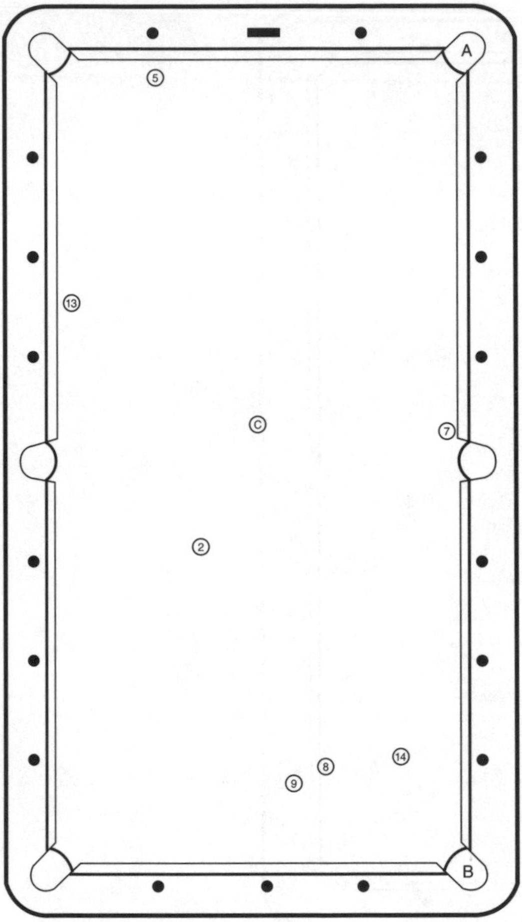

Diagram 43. You
have stripes.

You can play cat-and-mouse
with your opponent for a long
time from here, as long as you
don't leave the cue ball between
the 7 and pocket A. His 7-ball is
parked in approximately the
worst place there is on a pool
table, all but impossible to make

anywhere but pocket B (and
that's no cinch; if he tries, he's
very likely to hit the opposite
side-pocket point on the rail).
Try to make the 13 with enough
left-hand draw to get back near
the 9; you risk very little if
you miss.

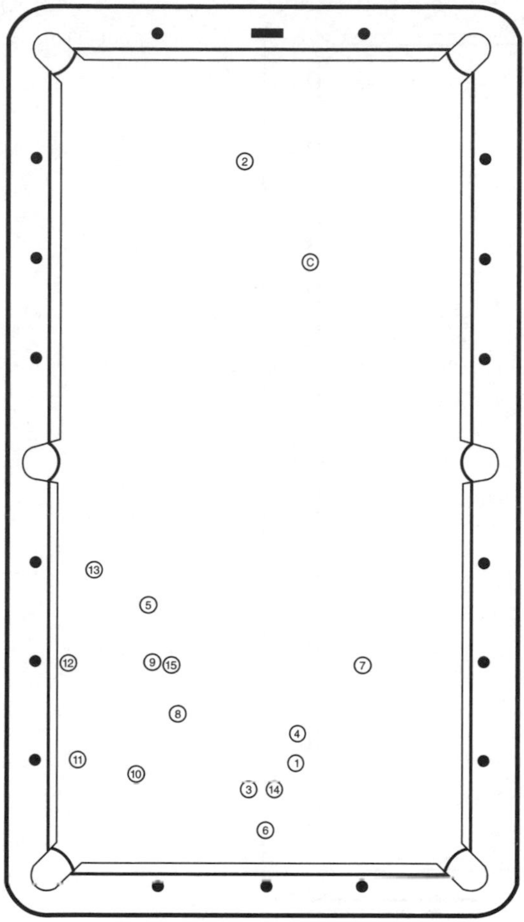

Diagram 44. The balls have just been broken.

This is a pretty typical break: some balls open, some still clustered. A good shooter could run out with either stripes or solids; the only problem balls in either case, the 3 or the 14 respectively, need be nudged only a ball's width below where they are now.

But there's an at least equally easy plan: pocket the 2-ball to claim solids, then roll the 7 down toward the bottom rail and leave your opponent on the wrong side of that mess with nothing to shoot at.

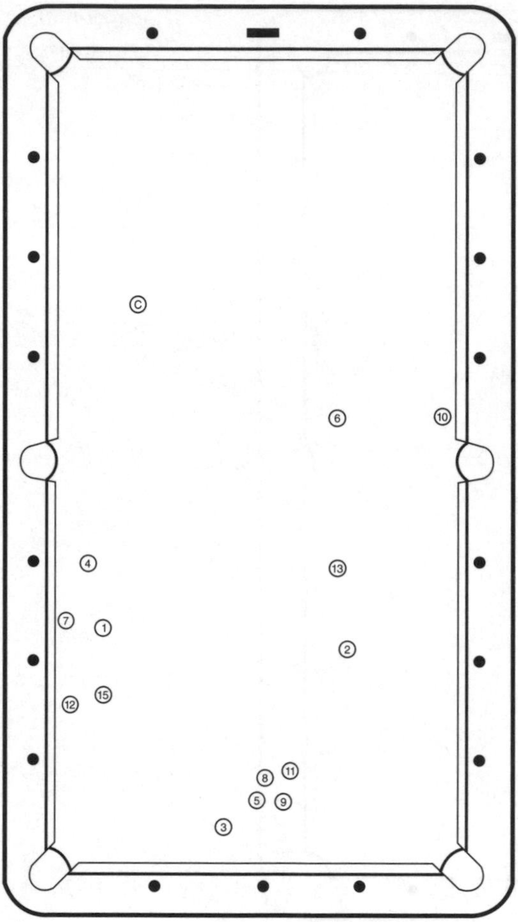

Diagram 45. You have stripes.

Deliver the 10 from its wretched position, banking it down-table, and draw the cue ball back to the end rail (just be careful not to leave your opponent a side-pocket shot at the 6). He has zilch to shoot at from way up there and can only lead you closer to the win.

How Would You Play This?

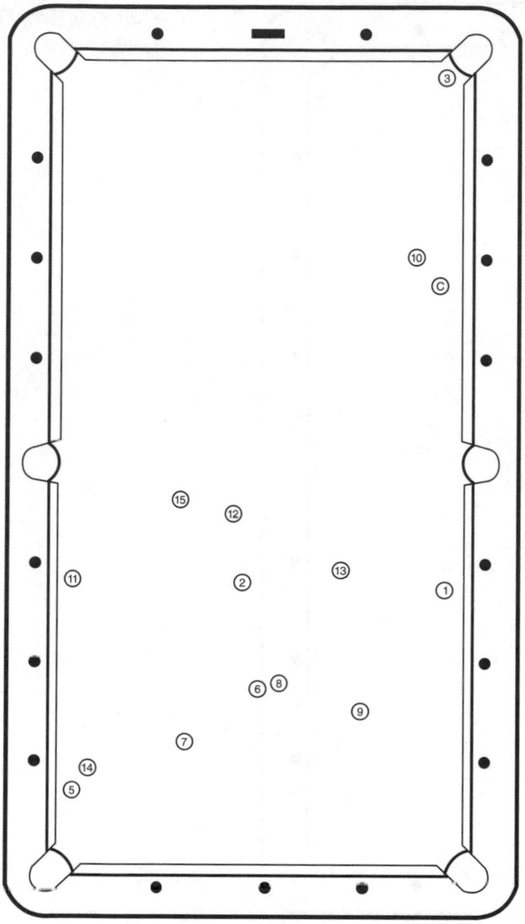

Diagram 46. You have solids.

Leave the 3-ball hanging where it is for now. It may be a good friend to you later; even better, it turns his 10 into a problem for him. Play the 1 with follow. Your next shot should be a gentle safety off the bottom of the 5-ball, bunting it to the side rail where it will be makable later, and park the cue ball on the end rail with juicy peace of mind.

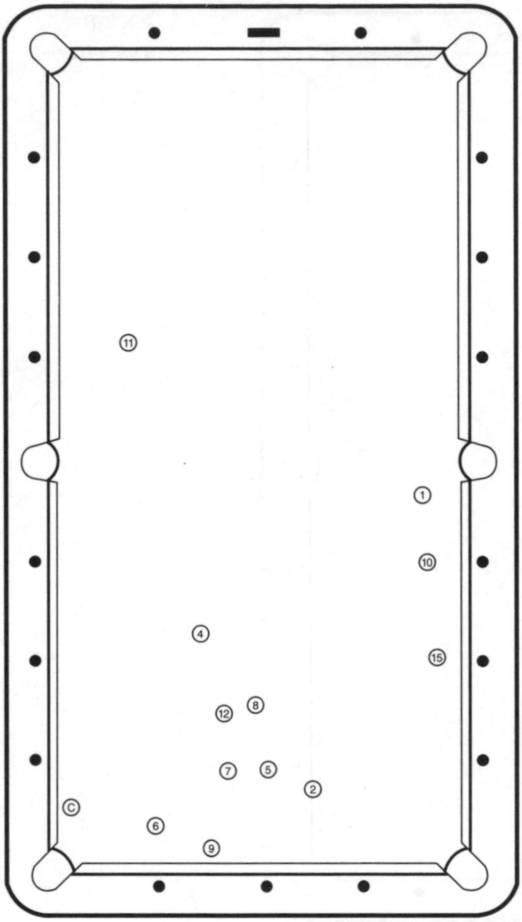

Diagram 47. You have stripes.

Yes, the 11 is the right shot—but you have to play it correctly. Roll it softly in the direction of the diagonally opposite corner pocket. Your objective is to leave the 11 near that pocket, in will-call position, and the cue ball on the end rail. Your opponent has no safety available that doesn't help you somehow.

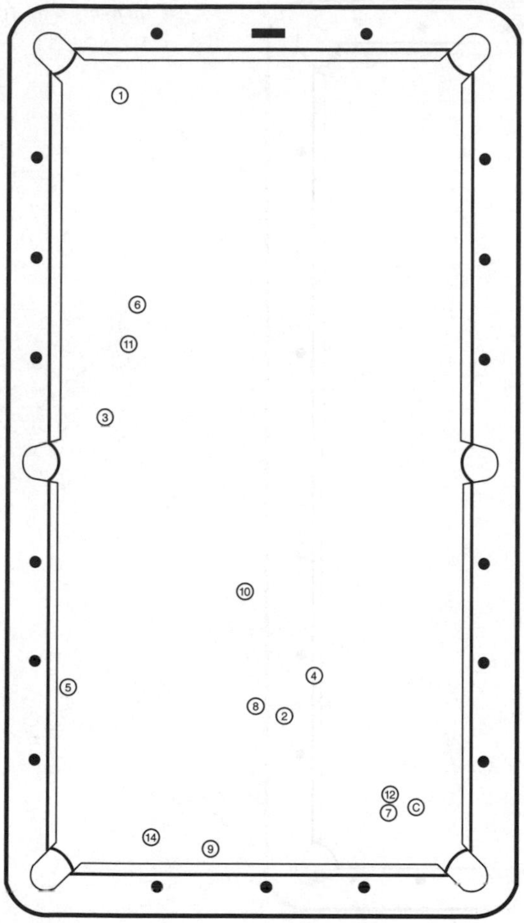

Diagram 48. You have stripes.

What could be simpler? Hit your cue ball exactly in its center and pop the 12 cleanly out of there at medium speed, leaving him stuck right up against his own 7. Where's he goin' from there?

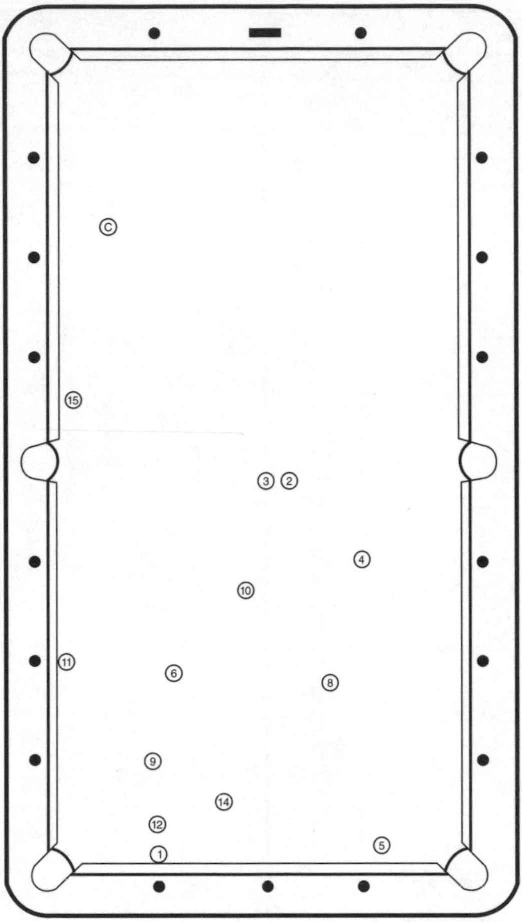

Diagram 49. You have solids.

You could try and play the 2-ball in the corner, going for the win. But it's not an easy shot, and if you miss, he'll probably have a chance for an easy run-out. Equally sound: drive the 2 into the 4 and draw the cue ball back in the area of the corner pocket.

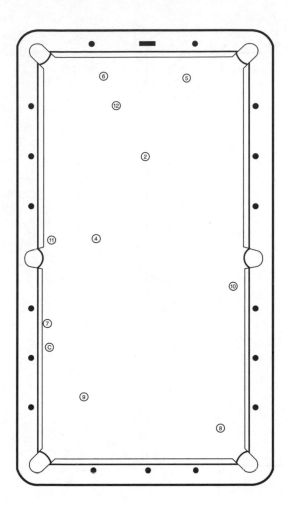

Diagram 50. You have stripes.

The 9 represents a do-or-die opportunity here. If you make it, in the corner nearest the 8, you're a strong favorite to run out the game; if you miss, with the balls this open, well. . . . It really depends on your comfort level with the shot. If you don't think you're odds-on to make it, roll it off the bottom rail and leave the cue ball down there. The most you should leave is a do-or-die for your opponent.

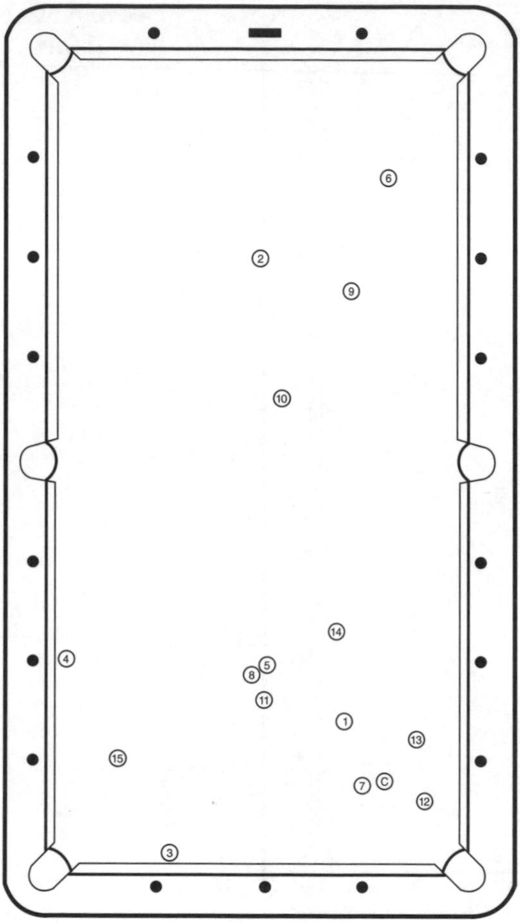

Diagram 51. The balls have just been broken.

It's going to be tough to find a good safety with the balls spread like this. So recognize that if you choose stripes, the only real problem confronting you is finding a pocket for the 9-ball. Try for position on it in the far diagonal corner pocket, by playing the 12 now with left-hand draw. You'll free the 8 when you shoot the 11, and you should be able to get position on the 11 off the 13. Learn to recognize your best-case scenarios; Eight-Ball's defensive aspects don't have to intimidate you out of the win.

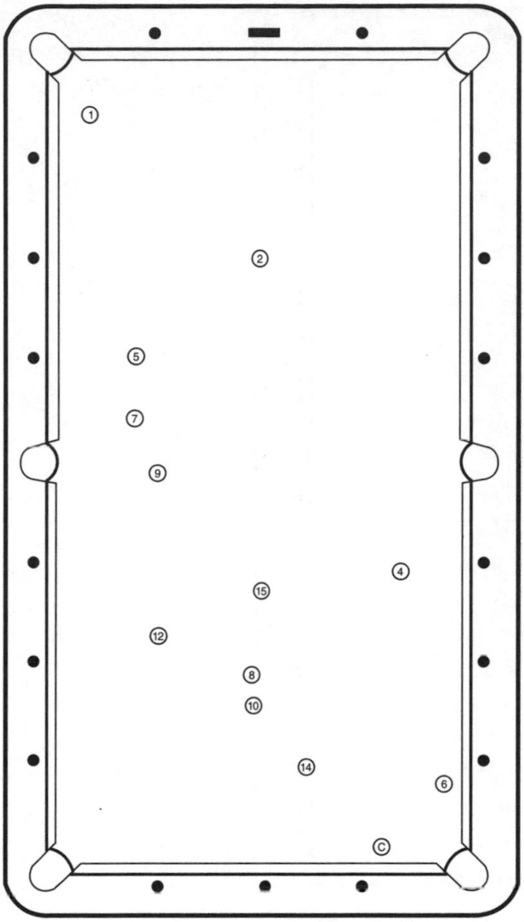

Diagram 52. You have stripes.

Every so often the game really stacks up against you, as it does here. You have two options—both tough—to bail this game out: cut the 15 in the side and hope you can run out from there, or shoot into the 14 and try to draw the cue ball back under the 6 for a safety. Fail at either and your opponent will probably run out. But *never give up on a game*; in pool, genius is often born of desperation.

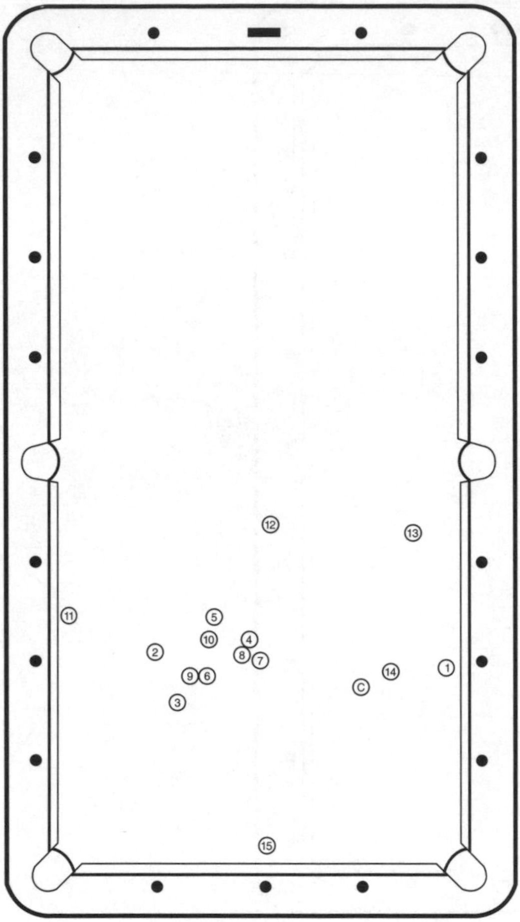

Diagram 53. The balls have just been broken.

Clearly this game's going to take a while. Although defensive strategies are available no matter which balls you choose, your job will be easier with stripes. Shoot either the 12 or the 13 (but not both), then bank the 14 off the bottom rail and leave the cue ball down there with the 15-ball.

Point to remember: *The most valuable aspect of Eight-Ball you can learn is patience.*

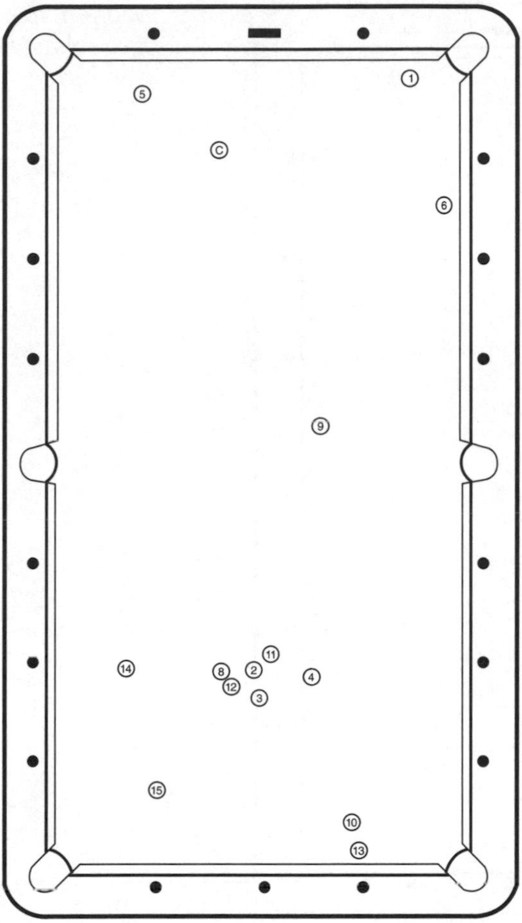

Diagram 54. You have solids.

You lucky dog! This game is tailor-made for you. Sink the 5, then *overcut* the 1 slightly to leave it in front of that near corner pocket and park the cue ball behind the 6. If your opponent fails to hit his striped balls from there, you get the cue ball anywhere on the table; at that point, choose the 2, so you can wiggle the 3-, 4-, and 8-balls into the clear. No excuse for not winning this game.

Point to remember: *Your thinking ahead need not necessarily involve the immediate pocketing of balls.*

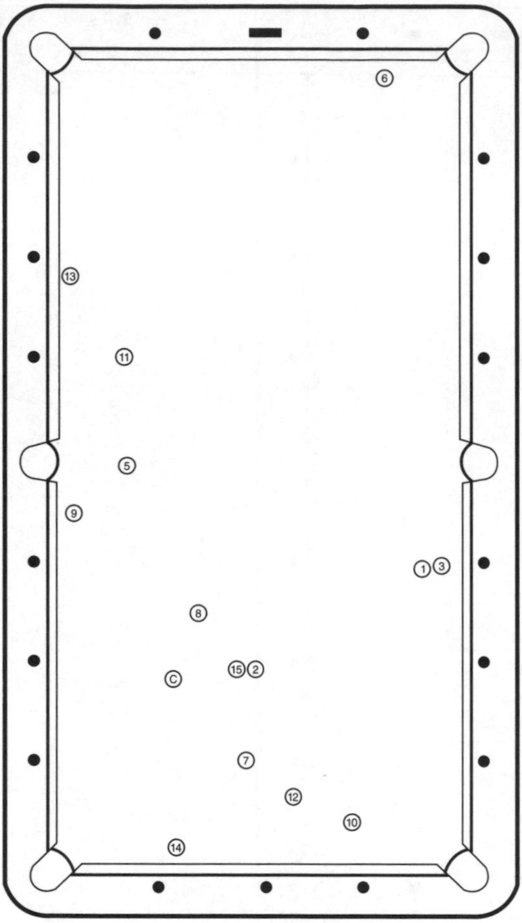

Diagram 55. You have solids.

And if you can wait one more inning, you should win with them. Cut the 5 in the side, with enough speed to go to the top rail and back down toward the 3; just shoot into the 3 so as to lock the cue ball against the 1. Should you ultimately be rewarded with cue-ball-in-hand, make your shot the 2-ball in the corner nearest the 6, and all your problems are solved.

Point to remember: *Two balls close together (such as the 1 and the 3) represent a powerful defensive opportunity.*

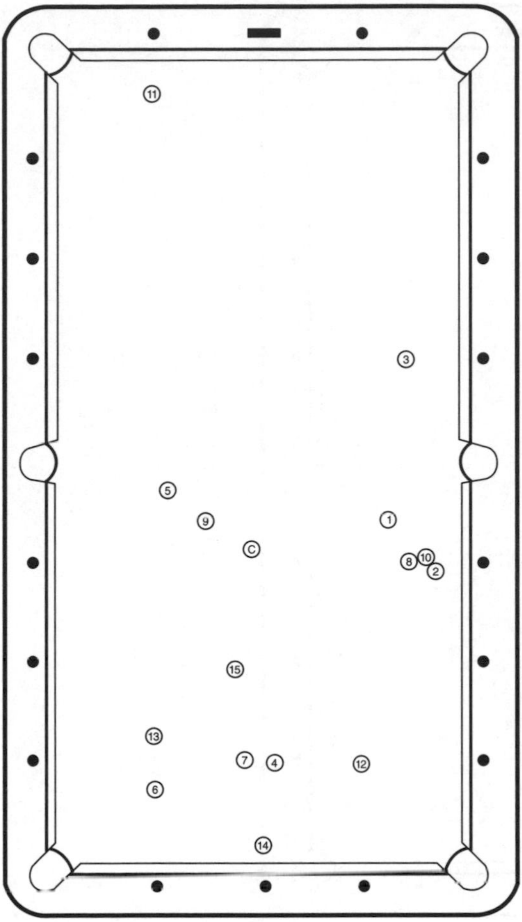

Diagram 56. The balls have just been broken.

Study this layout carefully, and you'll see a run-out possibility with solids. If you shoot the 1 into that side now, you'll separate that three-ball cluster and free your 2 *and* the 8. Why take that chance? Because the position of the 5- and 3-balls makes it certain you'll have an easy next shot no matter how those three balls separate for you.

Point to remember: *Plan on a nearby safety-valve shot when you separate clusters, whenever possible.*

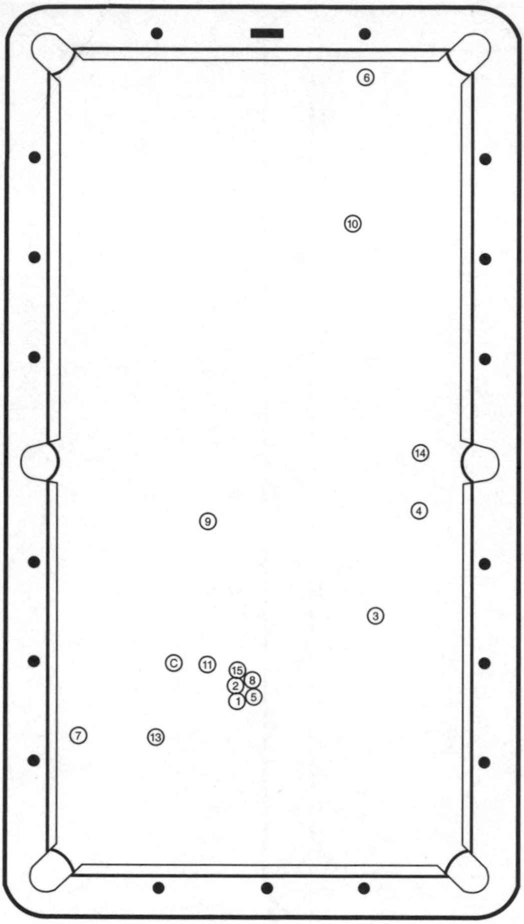

Diagram 57. You have stripes.

And it's not as bad as it might seem. Once the 13-ball is gone, you can get two-rail position on the 11 (using left-hand draw) to separate the still-clustered balls, freeing your 15 and 8. The 14-ball acts as your safety valve.

Point to remember: *Think ahead as far as you feasibly can.*

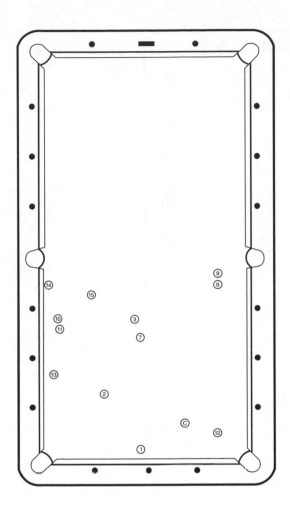

Diagram 58. You have stripes.

Your opponent has committed one of the most common mistakes in the game: he's run off three of his balls without winning. In effect, you're now leading 7–4, because that's how many defensive weapons you potentially have. Sacrifice one of those now, the 12, and get the cue ball someplace where you can bunt the 9 to a rail and leave your opponent—you guessed it—behind the proverbial 8-ball. If you get ball-in-hand, use it to separate the 11 from the 10 and create another hook that hides your opponent from his remaining balls.

Point to remember: *Beware, beware, beware of run-outs you can't finish.*

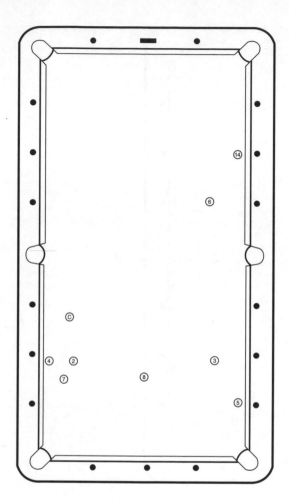

Diagram 59. You have solids.

You should definitely win this—so much so that you don't even have to make anything here. Just bunt the 4 and snooker your opponent on his last ball. If you get ball-in-hand, you won't have to deal with the tricky position you now need to make the 7. If you'd rather run the balls, play the 4 and move the 2 over so you have the 7 next—and try for a sequence that doesn't leave the 6 for last; you don't want to leave your opponent close to his ball.

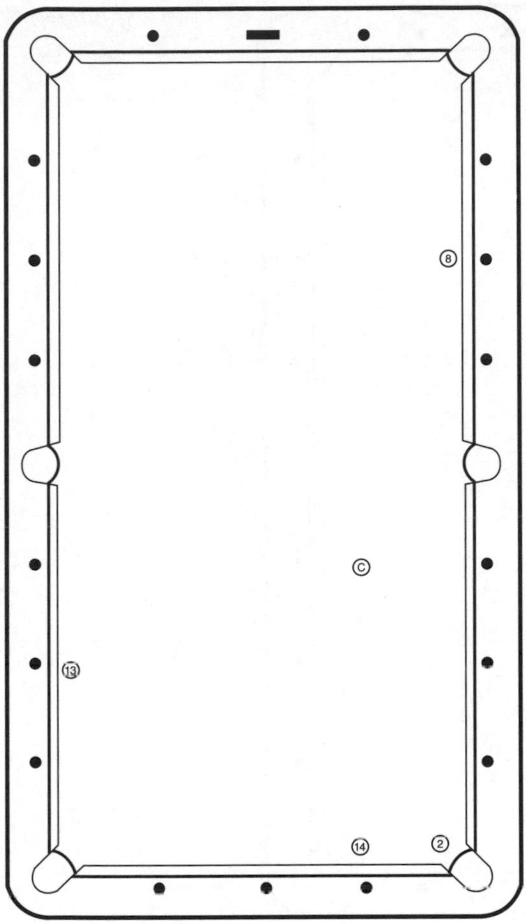

Diagram 60. You
have stripes.

In this scenario you have two
choices: (a) play a soft safety off
the 14-ball and try to hide your
opponent on the 2 or, even better, (b) make the 2 for him by

banking your 13 into it and
drawing your cue ball down
toward a position nearly parallel
with the 8 on the opposite rail.

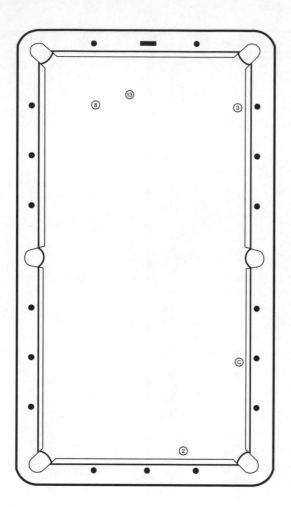

Diagram 61. You have solids.

If you shoot the 3-ball, position for the 2-ball is way too difficult; if you try cutting in the 2 and miss, you'll probably give the other guy a decent shot at his last ball and the game. So bank the 2 instead, and leave the cue ball in that area. You'll probably leave him nothing; both your balls will be in the vicinity of the 8-ball, and that should win.

How Would You Play This?

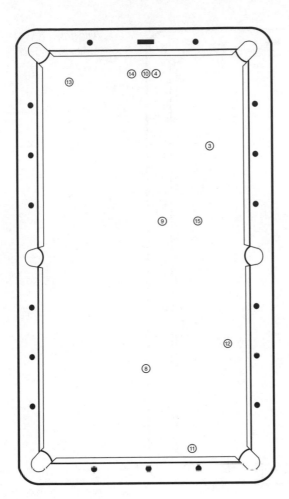

Diagram 62. You have stripes and your opponent just scratched.

I figured you deserved an easy one. You're entitled to shoot any ball on the table here, so make it the 14 and free up your 10. The point worth remembering is, you don't want to use so much finesse on the shot that you fail to drive the 10 free of the 4; use enough speed to drive it at least a ball's width closer to the end rail than it is now.

Point to remember: *The speed of the ball you're liberating should be part of your plan.*

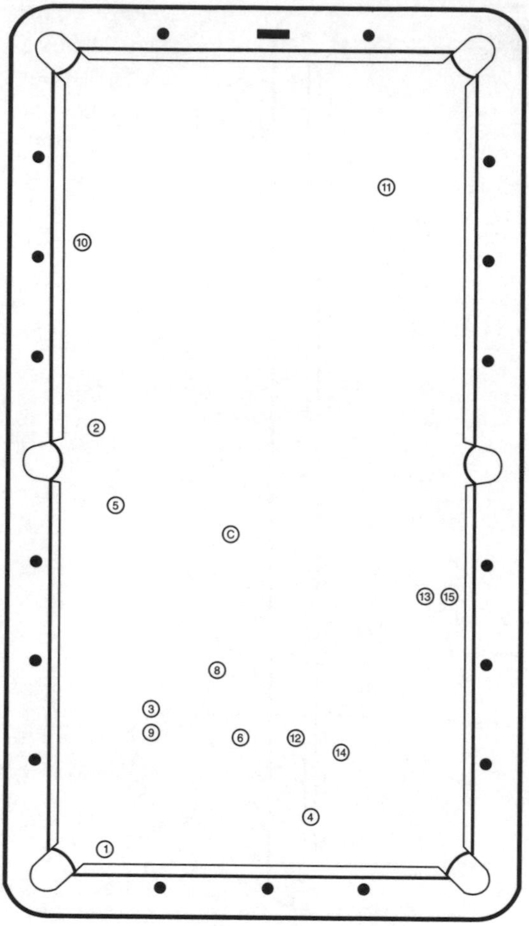

Diagram 63. The balls have just been broken.

It's probably worth the gamble to take solids and play the 5-ball, with a bit of left English so you can separate the 3- and 9-balls *now.* The positions of the 1 and 4 make it fairly certain that you'll have a shot no matter how you separate those two balls— not a cinch, but still your best chance to win outright with the balls this open. There is no handy way to move the 9 if you choose stripes.

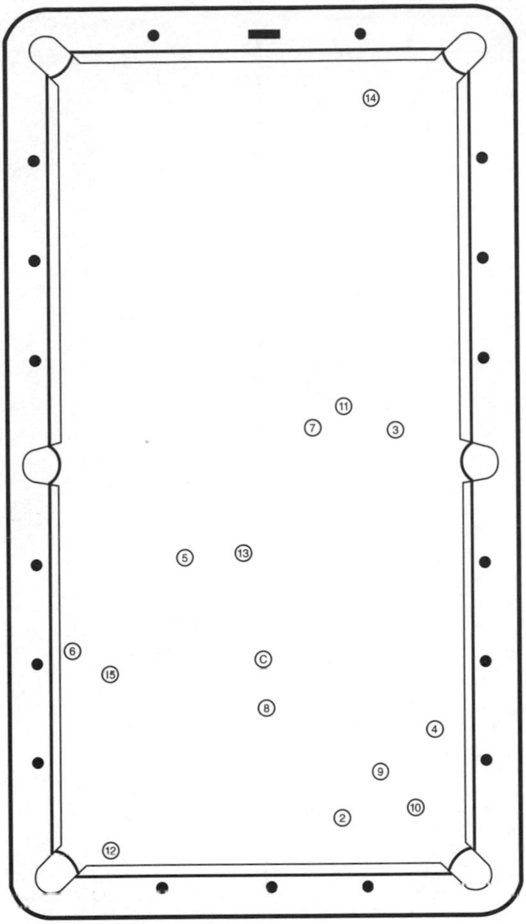

Diagram 64. The balls have just been broken.

With a run-out available either way, and very few defensive safeties apparent, just decide what suits you best. If you don't mind the 9-10 combination, and it's not hard, stripes are nearly as easy to run out as solids. If you want to play this defensively, play the 13 in the far corner with follow and hang the 14 up in the pocket that is closest to it. Your opponent will then have to make the 6—no bargain—to win.

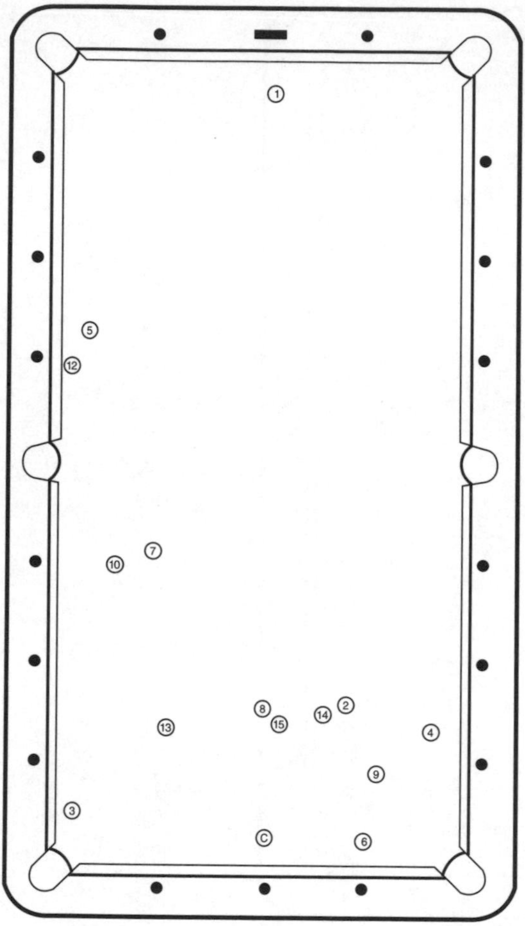

Diagram 65. The balls have just been broken.

There's a run-out with the solids if you want it; your 5 can be made but his 12 can't (at least, not until you move your 5). If you're not confident of the run-out, pocket the 6 and then roll softly under the 3, hiding your opponent from all the balls.

Point to remember: *Be alert for situations like the 5 and the 12, where yours goes but the other guy's doesn't; they're a big potential advantage.* (In this situation, you'll probably want to save the 5-ball for late in your sequence.)

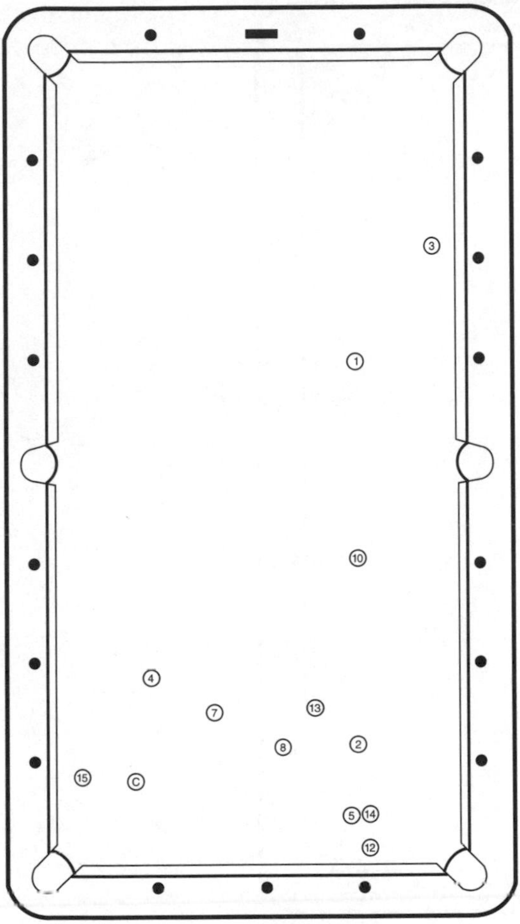

Diagram 66. You have stripes.

Why make the 12? You don't have a handy way to free your 14 anyway—or do you? The finesse play here is to bunt the 12 near, but not into, the closest pocket, using just enough speed to nudge the 14 loose. Ideally, your opponent will be frozen to your 14, too, but even if he's not, you should have him "in jail."

Point to remember: *Don't pocket balls before you have a plan for solving your remaining problems.*

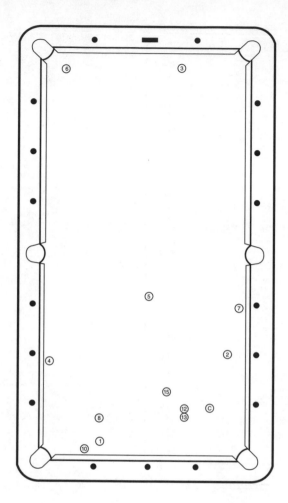

Diagram 67. You have stripes.

You *might* be able to make the 13-10 combination, by sending the 13 between the 1 and the rail—but do you want to bet the game on it? Much better to shoot the 13 into the 1, taking it out of the immediate area, and leaving the cue ball stuck on the 12. That solves all your problems and should win the game for you.

Point to remember: *Don't be overeager to pocket balls when there are less risky things to do.*

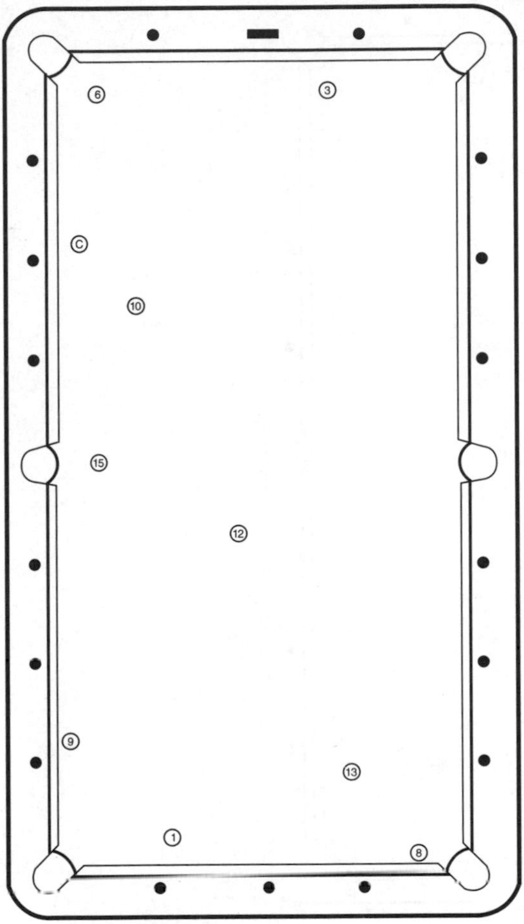

Diagram 68. You have stripes.

Looks like you got lucky and your opponent couldn't finish his run-out. What ball do you begin with? None of them. Just drive the 10 straight ahead and stick the cue ball; two balls have him hooked on the 8. This is another extension of the concept in Diagram 67.

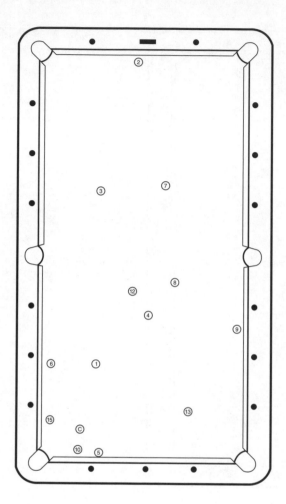

Diagram 69. You have stripes.

Looks like you goofed up, didn't follow my advice, and pocketed some stripes without getting the job finished, falling short of viable position on the 10-ball. Your best chance to bail this game out is a familiar move to players of the difficult pool game called One-Pocket: draw off the side of the 15 and bring the cue ball back against (or—even better—under) the 10.

Point to remember: *Don't panic when things go wrong; you will often have more options than you think.*

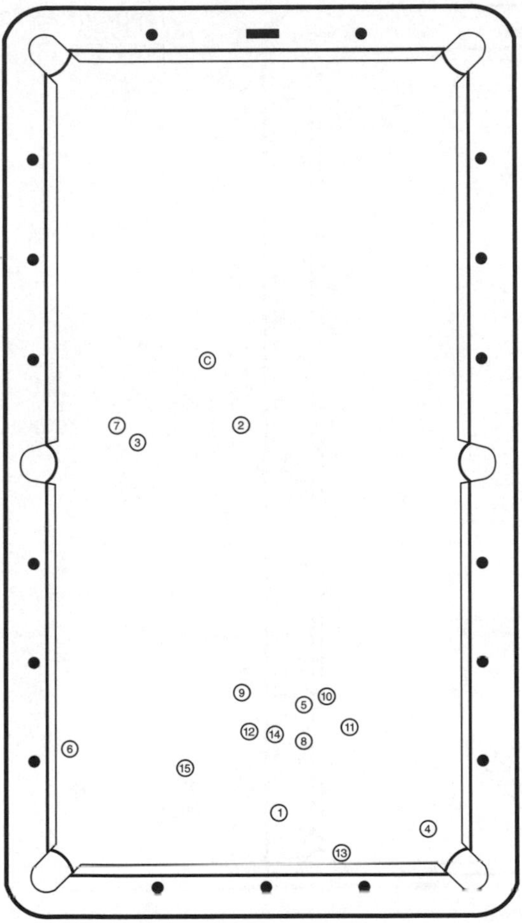

Diagram 70. The balls have just been broken.

Obviously your choice is solids—but make it the right number of solids: one. Pocket the 7 with enough force to send the 3 down near the pocket closest to your 6, stopping your cue ball right there. Then play off the far side of the 2 and leave the cue ball near or on the end rail. Your opponent has nothing—especially since you'll have both corner pockets protected—and his attempt will probably free your 5.

Point to remember: *Don't be greedy. Be patient.*

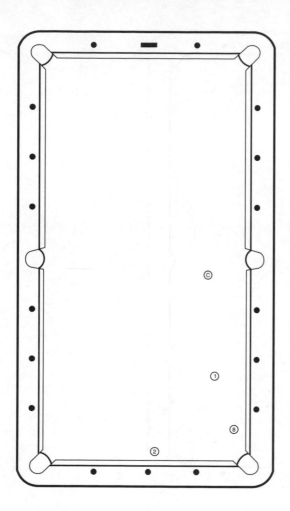

Diagram 71. You have solids.

It'll take a circus shot for you to win outright from here. You could try banking the 1 in the diagonally opposite corner, and parking your cue ball on the bottom rail with your 2. But if you're willing to wait one more inning, there's an easier tactic: drive your 1 into the bottom rail with enough speed that it rebounds and kicks the 8 all the

way up-table, hopefully near the center of the other end rail. The cue ball should end up close to your balls but far from your opponent's.

Point to remember: *When you simply can't win, you simply must keep the other guy from winning.*

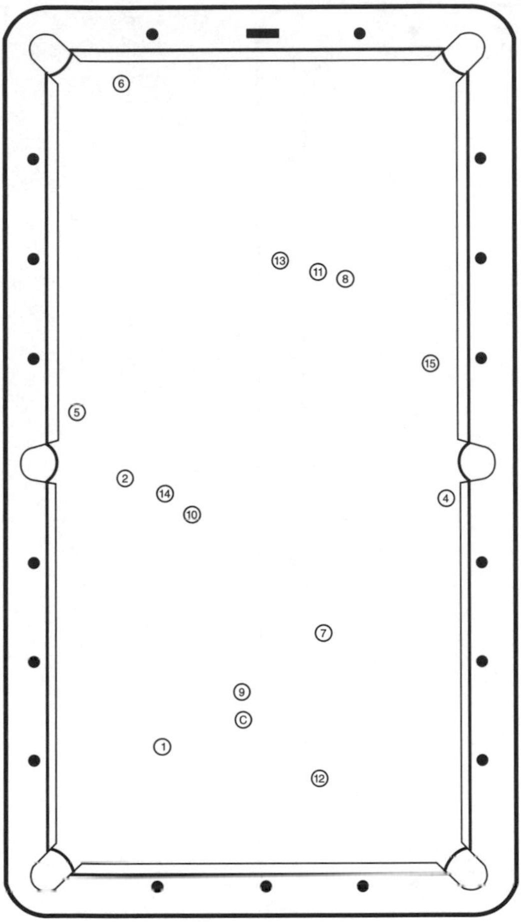

Diagram 72. The balls have just been broken.

While solids seem less desirable, because of the stinky position of the 4, they're still quite playable if you deal with the 4 early. Use the 1 to put your cue ball between the 4 and the 15 (but do avoid the side pocket), or shoot the 7 in the side to gain position for the 4 in the near corner. Yes, stripes would be the easier choice, but if the 12 were someplace else and solids were the only viable choice, now you know how to handle them.

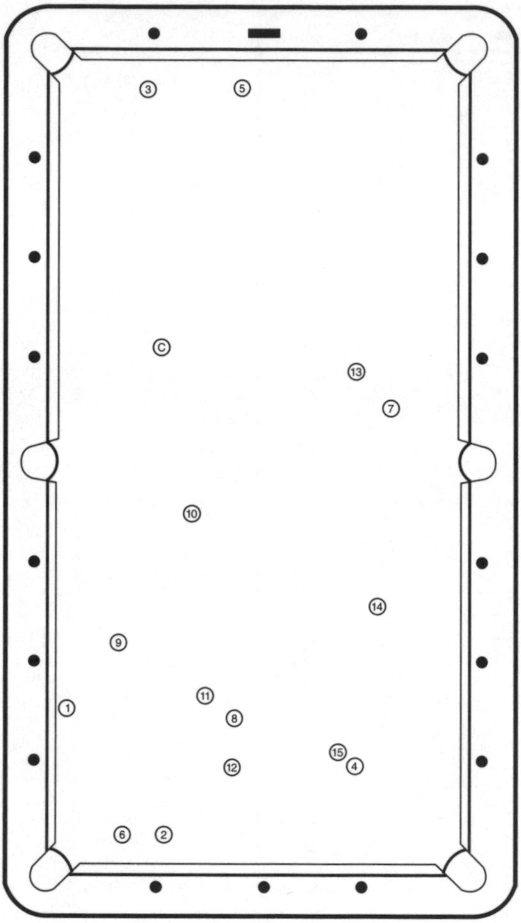

Diagram 73. The balls have just been broken.

Whaddya lookin' at? Under current rules, that can't-miss 15-4 combination is perfectly legal to shoot so as to acquire solids for yourself, and every other solid after that is open and available.

By all means, make sure that you and your opponent agree on the rules before you begin any Eight-Ball game or session—then take full advantage of those rules.

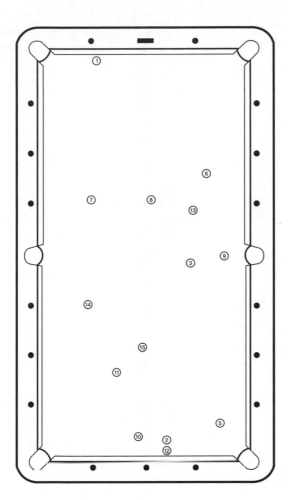

Diagram 74. You have solids and your opponent just scratched.

Start with the 2-ball; otherwise position for it will be way too tricky. Put your cue ball down under the 10, cut the 2 thinly into the corner, and send the cue ball up-table for the 6 and the 1.

Point to remember: *Problems should be dealt with sooner rather than later. It's like life.*

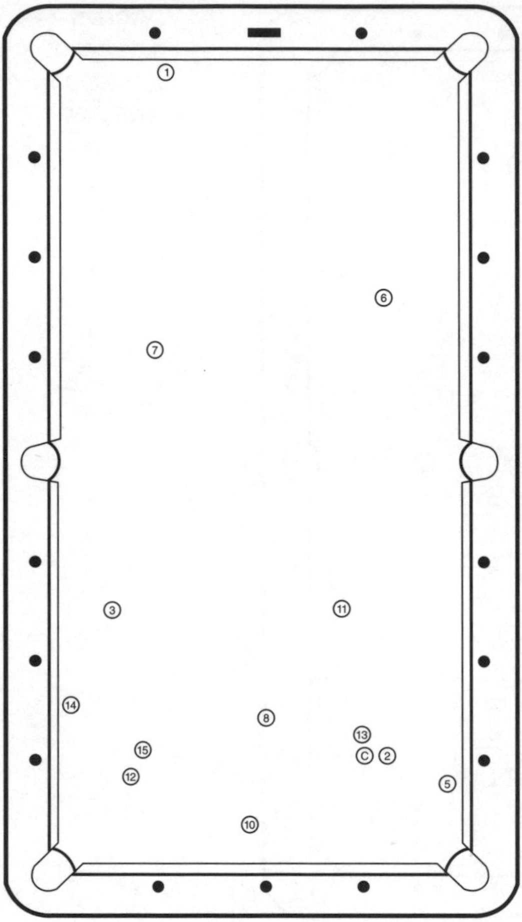

Diagram 75. You have stripes.

Are you sure you want to make that 10? Don't do it unless you've got a sensible plan for getting position on the 13 (the problem of the 15 is solved by playing the 14 softly just before it). The safest play of all is to hang the 10 up in that corner pocket so that your opponent has absolute zilch, and do battle from there. As Elaine said to Benjamin in *The Graduate*, "I don't want you to leave without a plan."

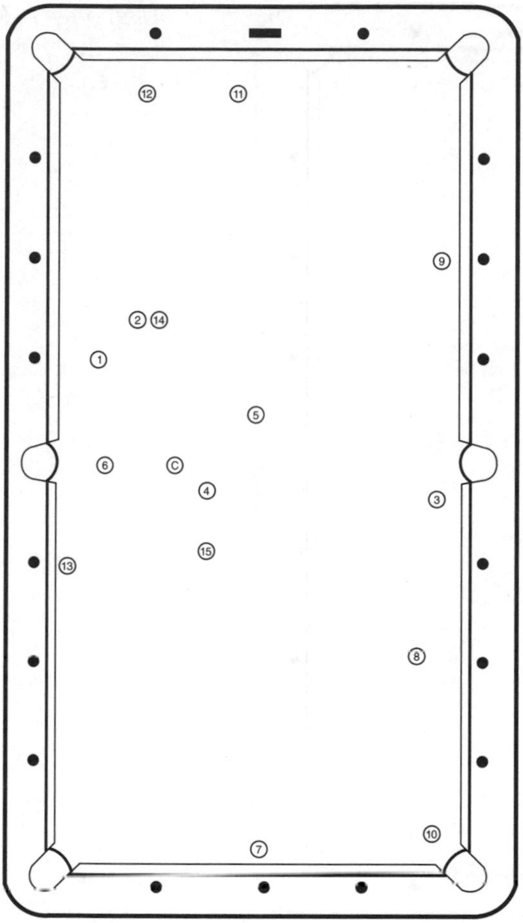

Diagram 76. The balls have just been broken.

Oh, don't those solids look tender and juicy? With that adorable little 6-ball right in front of you, and all the rest loose and mostly close by? They look great until you start thinking about where the 8-ball will go (right now there's *no* ready place for it). A quick hike around the table would've shown you that stripes were easily the better choice.

Point to remember: *Inspect your layout from all directions.*

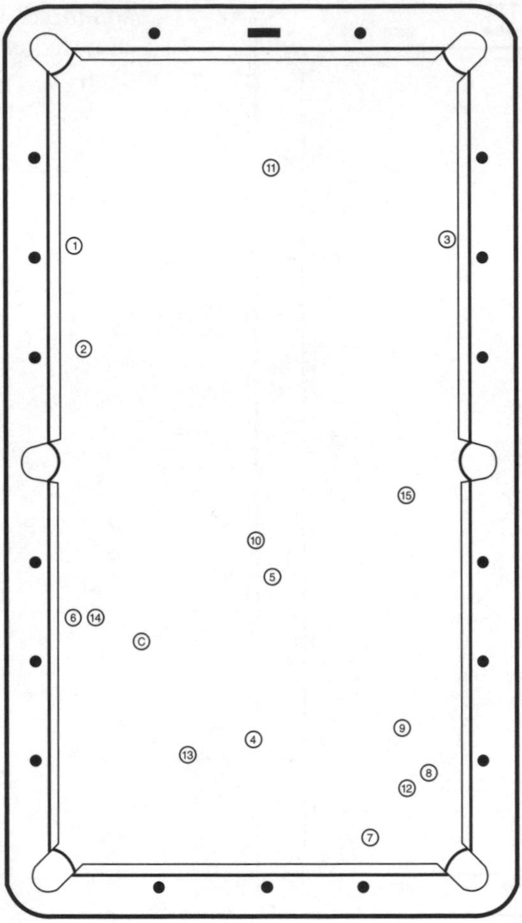

Diagram 77. The balls have just been broken.

A good player could run out going either way here but would probably look with disdain at the 1 and the 2 on the same rail when there's something easier to do. While the 8 looks like it's surrounded by stripes, just playing the 12 softly now will nudge the 8 toward the rail, opening up the table for you.

Point to remember: *Your first option should be to make things as easy on yourself as you can.*

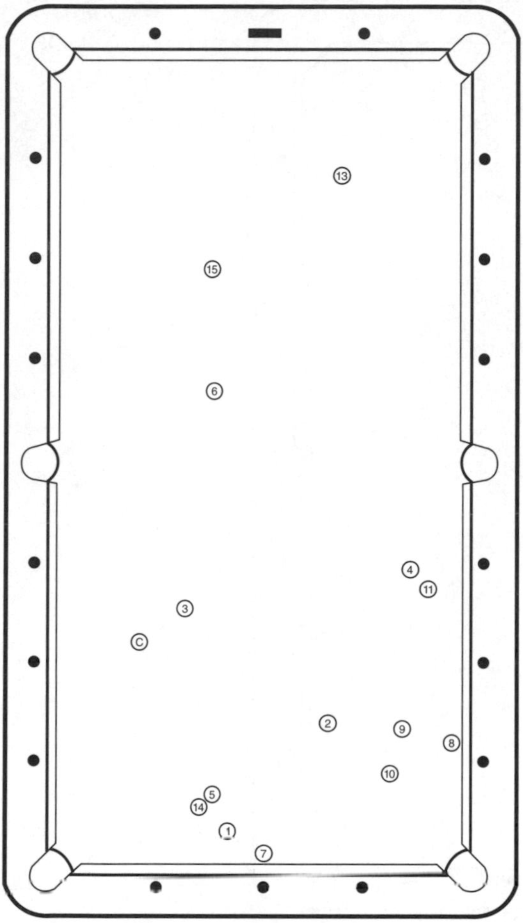

Diagram 78. The balls have just been broken.

Shoot the 13 with no more than medium speed. If you miss, you should leave very little with all those balls tied up down-table. If you make it, you should be more or less in line with the 15 and the 6; knock the former into the latter, sending them both down-table to confuse things further. If you can draw your cue ball back near the end rail, your opponent should have nothing more than a migraine.

Point to remember: *Think damage control when the game is not yet winnable.*

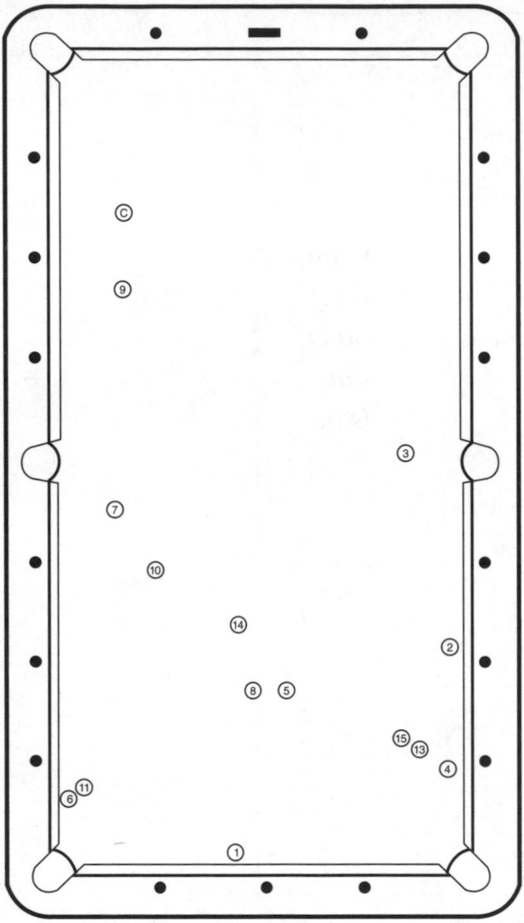

Diagram 79. You have solids.

It looks like you want to shoot the 3-ball in the side so you can send the cue ball down to get some breathing room for your 2 and 4—but don't. Play the 4 softly and leave his 13 and 15 tied up; if you miss, the cue ball is safely on the bottom rail with nothing open. If you make the 4, your next shot should be the 2, going the other way. Leave the 1 on the rail for when you use the 7 to separate the 11 and the 6. This provides you with two lessons in one.

Point to remember 1: *Leave your opponent's balls tied up whenever possible; that's a problem for him to solve, not you.*

Point to remember 2: *A lone ball on the bottom rail, until all your other balls are open, can be the same friend in Eight-Ball that it is in Straight Pool.*

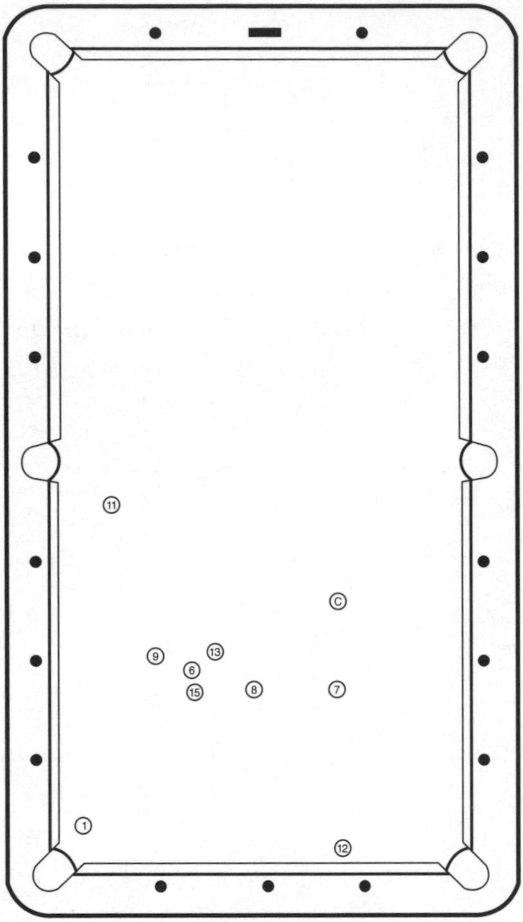

Diagram 80. You have stripes.

Don't shoot that 11-ball, because none of your other stripes has a logical path to a pocket yet. Instead, use your 15 delicately to make your opponent's 1. You'll move the 6, freeing your 9 and 13, and he should be hooked on both the 6 and the 7.

Point to remember: *Making your opponent's ball for him, before he can use it for position, can be a powerful weapon in your arsenal.*

3

NINE-BALL

This is the game you currently see the pros playing on cable TV. But even if you're a fan of televised pool, there's still a chance you may be seeing this game in an incorrect light. It may look simplistic or seem like a matter of luck at first, and while it can be just that now and then, Nine-Ball is really a difficult, complex game of angles.

Unlike Straight Pool or Eight-Ball, Nine-Ball confronts you and your opponent with the same target, the lowest-numbered ball remaining on the table. Thus the diagrams you'll see here don't deal with which ball to shoot; instead it becomes a question of where you want to put that ball—and, if no pocket is available for it, what else you want to do with both that ball and the cue ball.

Should a diagram be captioned "The balls have just been broken" in this section, that means you have the option of rolling the cue ball anywhere on the table you wish if you don't like your shot, and challenging your opponent to either shoot your leave himself or allow you to. (You must make a legal hit on your second try, or you surrender cue-ball-in-hand to your opponent, as you do on any foul.)

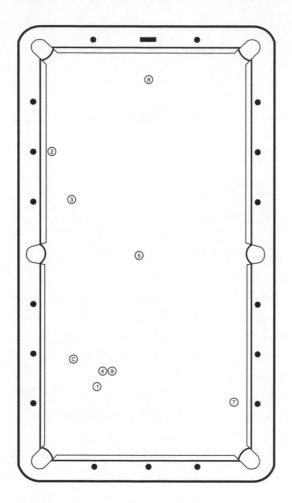

Diagram 81.

The 1 is makable here—but why bother? There's no way to deal with the 4 right now anyway. So use that worthless 4-9 tandem to your advantage, hiding the cue ball behind it as you drive the 1 out of there. Best of all: play that safety with enough draw to nudge the 4 maybe half a ball's width, so it will ultimately be makable for you when your opponent fails to hit the 1.

Point to remember: *When the higher-numbered balls aren't all open, stop thinking in terms of pocketing open shots you have now.* It's senseless.

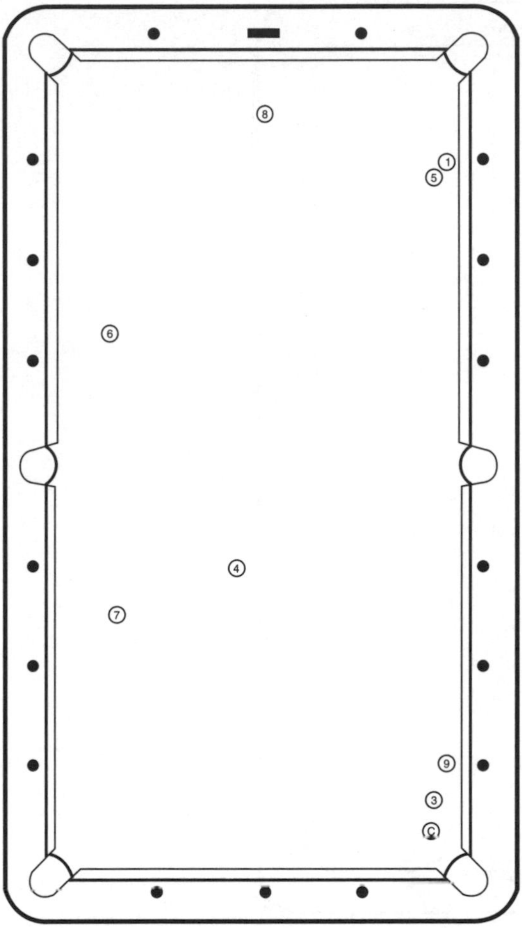

Diagram 82. The balls have just been broken.

There's very little point in trying to hit the 1-ball here. Even if you did, and the odds are very much against it, you wouldn't make anything and you'd leave the cue ball close to the 1 for your opponent's easy play. So nudge the 3 over under the 9, as your legal roll-out. That way, when you surrender ball-in-hand to your opponent one inning from now—he's almost certain to play you safe again, from here— at least you know he can't get out directly.

Point to remember: *When the game is stacked against you like this, you must resort to limiting what your opponent can do.*

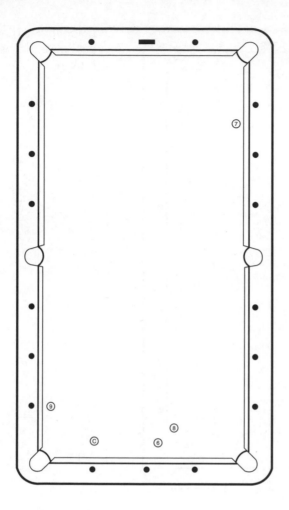

Diagram 83.

Here's an extremely common opportunity. Normally you don't want to move a second object ball that's already open, but here you do. Make it a point to drive the 8 toward the side rail as you sink the 6. It will simplify things considerably when it comes to making the 7; now you no longer have to draw your cue ball the length of the table for position.

Point to remember: *No matter how capable you are, avoid leaving yourself hard things to do.* The player who does the best job of simplifying is the player who figures to win.

Diagram 84.

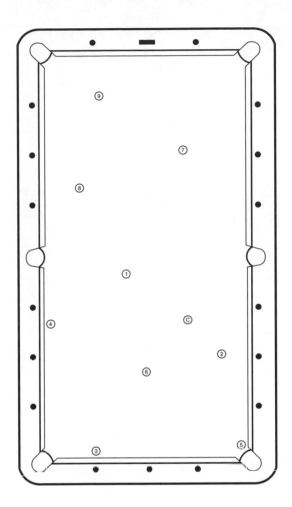

Of course you play the 2-5 combination. The point to be learned—a subtle but important one—is that you don't want the 2 to touch the rail in front of the 5. While that technique does increase the target area, it also makes it all too easy for the 2 to slide off a few inches on that bottom rail, to someplace unmakable and worthless. Cue-ball control is easier my way, too. Learn this; it comes up all the time. (If you have the 9 where the 5 is now, on the other hand, using the rail first with the 2 increases your target area, so by all means do that. You don't care where the 2 ends up if you're winning the game with that shot.)

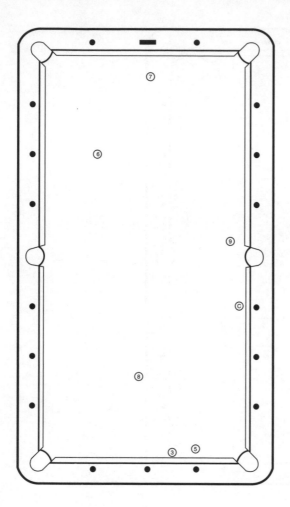

Diagram 85.

Yes, you play off the side of the 3, with high left English, to carom in the 5. What's equally important is cue-ball speed. With the right amount, your cue ball will travel up-table past the 9-ball, and the 3-ball will take a two-rail route to where you have an easy combination shot on the 9 for the win. This is very advanced, but the concept isn't too complex.

Point to remember: *If you're going to move more than one ball, chart the flight of all the balls you do plan to move.*

Diagram 86.

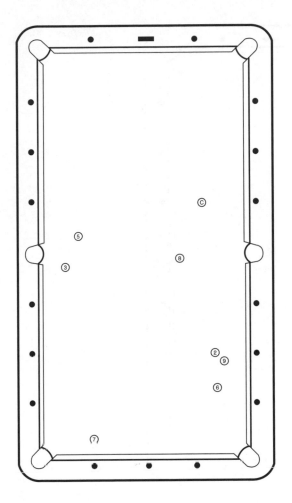

It takes pretty fair cue-ball control, but the right shot is to bank the 2 out of there with draw and try to stick the cue ball behind the 6 and 9. The 2-6 combo is strictly for suckers.

Point to remember: *Resolve right now to forget about off-angle combination shots with more than a few inches between the balls (unless there's simply no other option).*

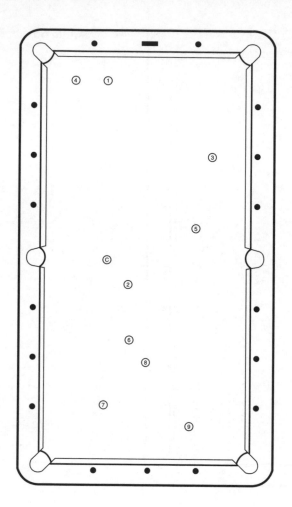

Diagram 87.

The 1 is do-or-die here. It's mak-able—but can you predict your cue ball's path with any cer-tainty? It would be wiser to play for some soft, simple hook involving the 4.

Point to remember: *If it looks like you're going to send the cue ball into balls that are already loose, look for something else to do.*

Diagram 88.

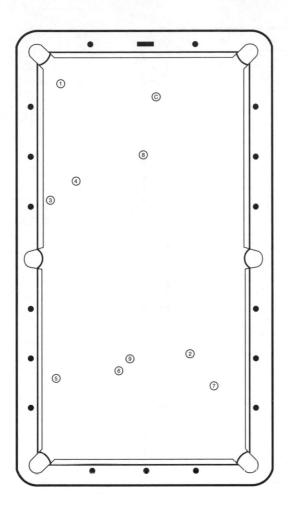

Here's another very common dilemma (although it defies precise diagramming). Let's say that there's barely room to sneak the 2 past the 7. Before you shoot the 1, determine what your confidence level is for that half-a-pocket shot. If it's not comfortably high, plan on position that lets you play defense using the 6-9 tandem to create a hook for your opponent.

Point to remember: *Don't shoot open balls without a plan that considers your strengths and weaknesses.*

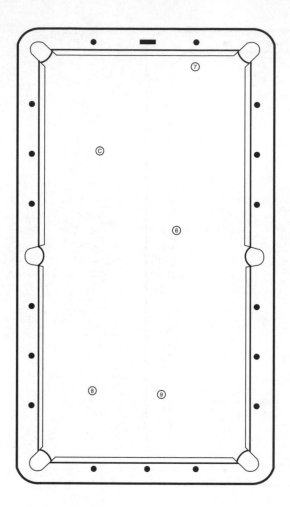

Diagram 89.

Many advanced players would choose to put the 6 in the corner instead of the side. Position for the 7 is simpler that way; you don't risk running your cue ball into the 9, and you're also guaranteed of distance between the cue ball and the 6 should you miss.

Point to remember: *Corner-pocket shots instead of side-pocket shots, when you have the choice, frequently increase your cue-ball options.*

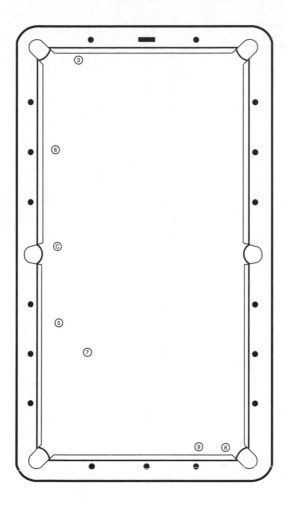

Diagram 90.

Your options here are more fertile than you might think. Note how the 8-ball increases your chances if you bank the 3 at that pocket (an advantage known as "sideboards" among players); and especially note the defensive potential of the 6.

Point to remember: *Any time you get a ball within, say, two balls' width of the long rail and two diamonds or less from the pocket, that's a big, big snookering opportunity, usually easy to reach.*

Diagram 91.

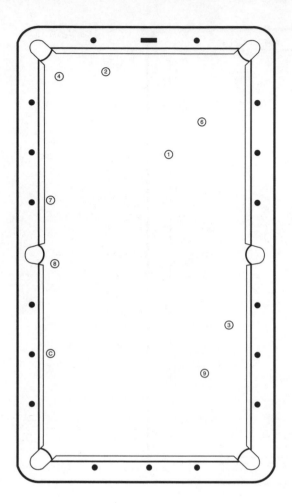

The 1 can't get by the 6; worse, if you drive it into the 6 at all, you're probably going to leave the cue ball relatively close to it. So cut it into the end rail with enough speed to take it back down-table, while your cue ball

hopefully slides behind the 4 or the 2 (it may not).

Point to remember: *When you can't be sure of hooking your opponent, think in terms of at least leaving him distance.*

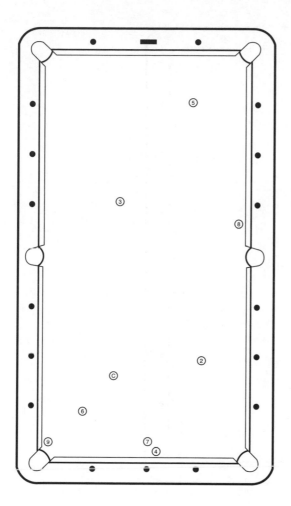

Diagram 92.

The balls are technically open here. But your bank on the 2 takes your cue ball away from, not toward, the 3; additionally, position from the 3 to the 4 is an extremely low-percentage proposition. So bank the 2-ball to miss on the far side of the pocket (not the near side; that's a very important distinction, in terms of defense) and try to get your cue ball to tickle the 4 and the 7 a bit farther apart. You'll solve the 4-ball conundrum, and leave your opponent long and shotless, if he can see the 2 at all, with the 9 very close to a pocket.

Point to remember: *You must think at least three balls ahead.*

Diagram 93.

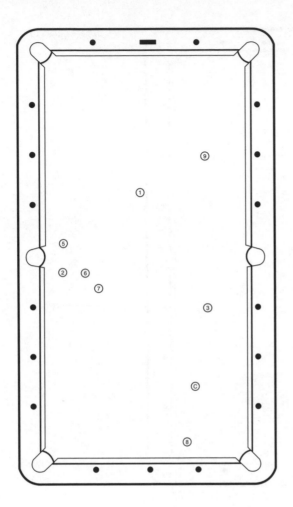

Again, the balls are open, and a top player could negotiate this as it lies. But notice that (a) the 5 and the 6 actually protect the 2 pretty well; your window for position on the 2 is actually quite small, and (b) the 2, 5, 6, and 7 represent a potential defensive wall for you to use in hiding the object ball, the cue ball, or both. I'd play off the far side of the 1, trying to bank it back down-table and hook my opponent behind those four balls.

Point to remember: *Not disturbing secondary object balls works defensively as well as offensively.*

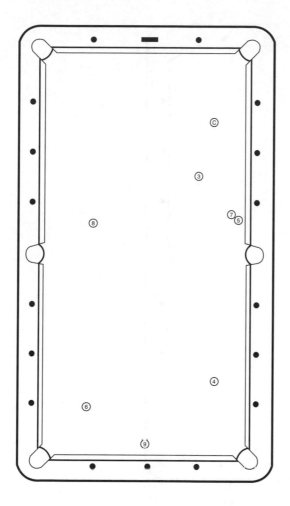

Diagram 94.

There's no open pocket for the 3-ball here, and that nasty 5-7 combination offers intriguing snookering possibilities. This is a good example of how to combine defense with offense: play the snooker, but with enough speed to separate the 5 and the 7 slightly, so you can negotiate them once your successful hook nets you ball-in-hand.

Point to remember: *Hooking your opponent is only of minimal value if problems still remain on the table; he knows that even if he doesn't complete a legal hit, you still aren't likely to run out.* Hooking him with all the balls open, however, will cause him great consternation indeed.

Diagram 95.

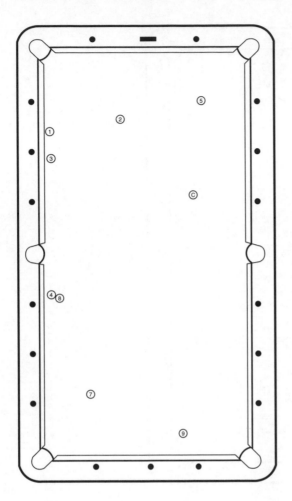

Similar to the concept just demonstrated. Maybe there's room to make the 1 here—but so what? The 4-8 combo will stymie you anyway. So drive the 1 out of there, sticking the cue ball at the point of contact, and be sure to use enough speed to drive the 1 off three rails; you've got a pretty natural angle to break up the 4-8 combination with the 1 at the same time you hook your opponent.

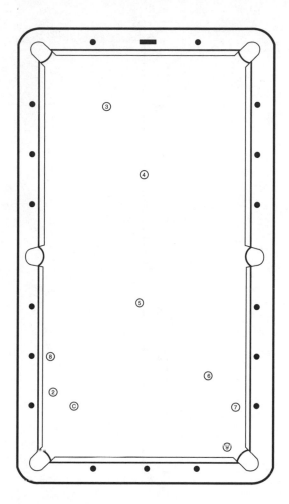

Diagram 96.

Toss your opponent a triple whammy like this and watch him turn the color of the cue ball: the right shot would normally be to play a billiard from the 2 to the 9. (Banking the 2 into the 9 is way too high a risk.) However, the position of the 8 means that you won't be able to drive the 2 out of the area should you miss the 9. So play into the rail, just in front of the 9, with high right English. You're trying to (a) successfully carom into the 9; (b) maybe pocket the 2 in the opposite diagonal corner; (c) snooker behind the 7-ball on the opposite rail if you don't pocket the 9-ball; or (d) possibly all three!

Point to remember: *Don't just decide you're going to try to sink the 9 out of sequence; think about all the other balls you have to move to do that.*

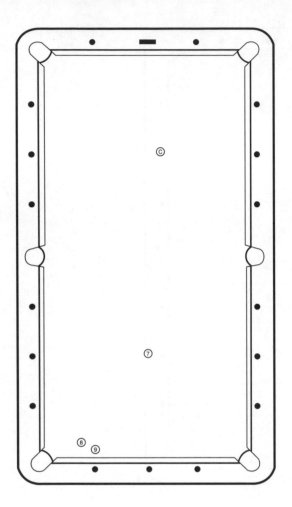

Diagram 97.

It'll take a circus shot to win out-right here—or, if you're willing to wait one more inning, a very easy one. Simply aim the center of the cue ball at the edge of the 7-ball and shoot with high center English. The resultant deflection off the 7 should take your cue ball to the side rail and then behind the 8, for a snooker and a win.

Point to remember: *You must learn the angles of cue-ball deflection off object balls, for all the various cue-ball hits (high, center, and draw).* They're one of the obvious keys to advanced pool.

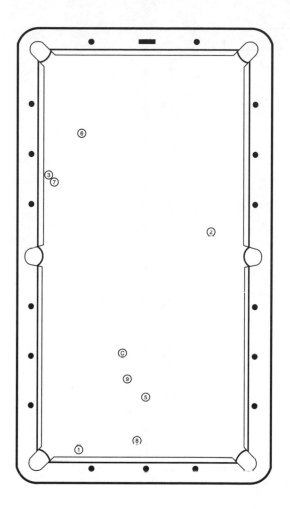

Diagram 98.

Because the 1 offers you a natural angle of approach to the wretched 3-7 tandem—*and* because the 2 is right across the way from that tandem—go ahead and play the shot that way. When there is no safety valve like this, and the next ball you need is part of a cluster that must be separated (for instance, if the 2 were where the 3 is now), you need *both* a natural approach to that cluster and a reasonably clear vision of where the clustered balls will be going. Otherwise, don't pocket anything; play defense.

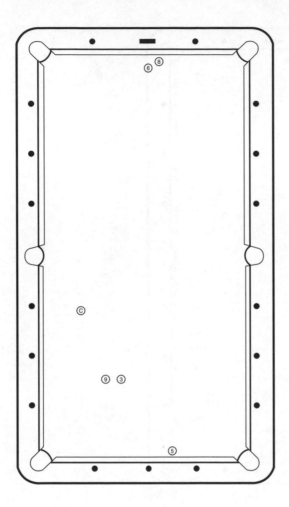

Diagram 99.

You may have a gift here (although, again, it's not easily diagrammed). Inspect the line between the edges of the 3 and the 9. If that line points to a pocket, you've got an easy carom shot. Even though the 3 is makable here, forget about it and try to pocket the 9 instead if it appears to be "on"—especially with that tricky position from the 5 to the 6.

Diagram 100.

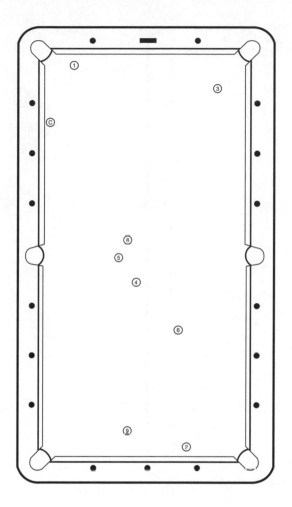

You've got at least two good strong safeties here: (a) feather the 1-ball, leaving it about in the middle of the end rail, and send your cue ball down-table, or (b) go in behind the 1 with high right English and hit the 1 rail-first, sticking the cue ball right there and driving the 1 down-table. Either way, the apparently innocent 4, 5, and 8 in center table become potent snookering weapons.

Diagram 101.

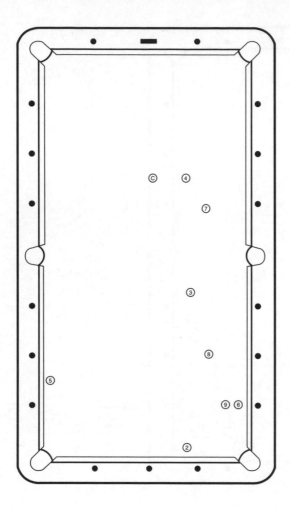

You wouldn't *believe* how many dumb players would play the 3-8-9 combination here, simply because it appears to line up visually. But with that much space between those three balls, it's close to a 10–1 proposition. It is wiser—and easier—by far to simply roll the 3-ball in behind the 6 and 9.

Diagram 102.

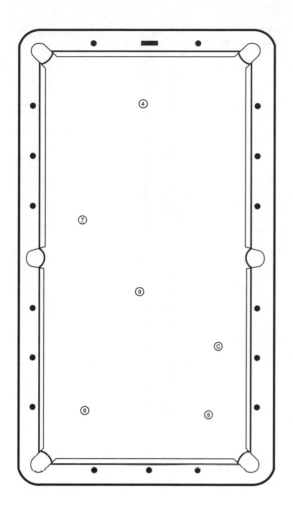

It's not as bad as it looks. The trick is to cut that 4 thin into the corner with an eye toward *over-*cutting the ball. That way, you either get a pocketed 4 with your cue ball moving easily back toward the 6, or a safety with distance. Most suckers will undercut the 4 here and leave something juicy.

Point to remember: *On thin cut shots, always try to err on the side of overdoing things (what players call missing on the professional side).*

Diagram 103.

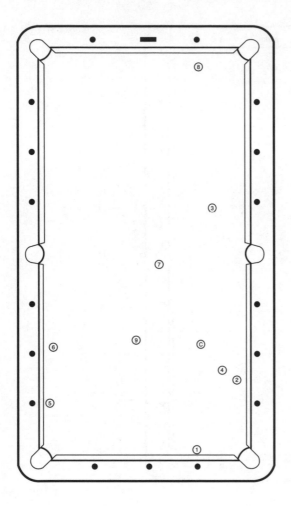

Can't really play a safety off either side of the 1 here; the 2 and the 4 block your cue ball's escape route on one side, the 6 on the other. But there's still a neat safety here: just shoot straight into the 1 with draw.

Execute this correctly and the 1 will stay right where it is—after double-kissing your cue ball the length of the table. Watch for this; it's more common than you might think.

Diagram 104.

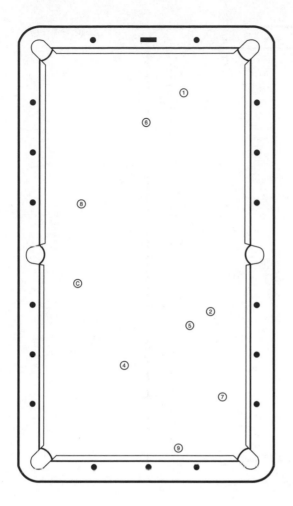

With the 7 blocking the 2's path, it's time to focus on one of the game's most important position routes, two rails out of the corner. You hit the 1 as diagrammed with low left English, and with enough force that the cue ball's *spin* is working for you as well as its speed. You're trying for a shot on the 2 in the side pocket nearest where the cue ball is now. Learn this pattern, and practice it at many different angles. It's invaluable, in all pool games.

Diagram 105.

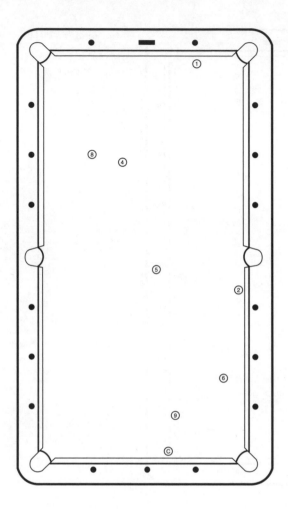

Unless you can massé the cue ball (which should thrill management in the room where you play), or curve it (with draw) between the 4 and the 8, you're not going to hit the 1 and are therefore a strong favorite to lose (though those first two options are valid if you have the skill).

We've looked at this concept before: try to roll the 9 someplace where it stymies the 6 (but, naturally, don't leave a combination shot on it).

Point to remember: *Damage control beats desperation nearly every time.*

Diagram 106.

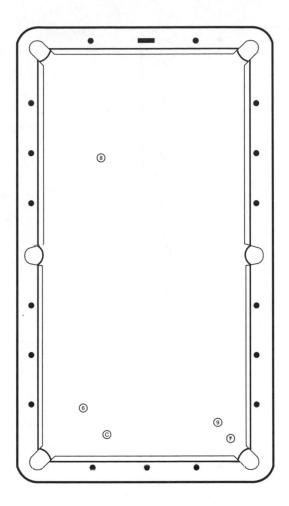

Don't be afraid of the thin cut shot in the far corner. At correct speed, you'll still be leaving distance and keeping the cue ball in the general area you need for position on the tricky 7. Again, think about overcutting this if you must miss; it won't come back as far that way. If you'd rather bank the 6 diagonally to the opposite corner, you want to miss it "short" (that is, on the long-rail side) rather than "long" for a better defensive leave.

Diagram 107.

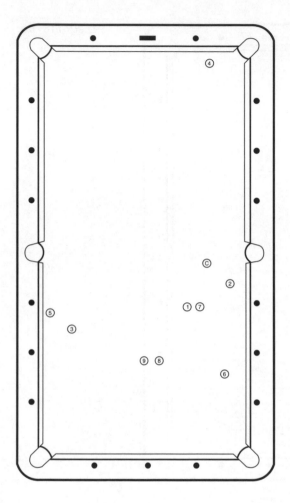

It's an elementary safety—just roll the 1 behind the 8 and 9— but notice how the 8 seems to guide the 1 to a good spot where it can knock in the 9. The safety is a certainty; the 1-9 combo, a high probability. Your call, and it depends on whom you're playing, how things are going, and how you feel about the shot generally.

Point to remember: *Learn to think all your options through, rather than firing on the first one you recognize.*

Diagram 108.

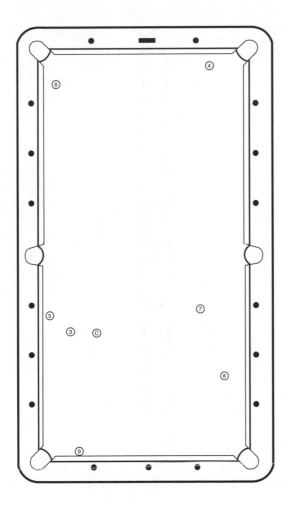

(Later in the same rack as shown in Diagram 107.) You can't bank that 3 in the side, so get acquainted with one of the game's more common safeties: cut the 3 thin enough to bank behind either the 7 or the 6; send your cue ball down near, and hopefully under, the 4. The shot carries the possibility of a hook on the object ball *and* on the cue ball *and* distance, too. Learn this move well, focusing on cue-ball speed.

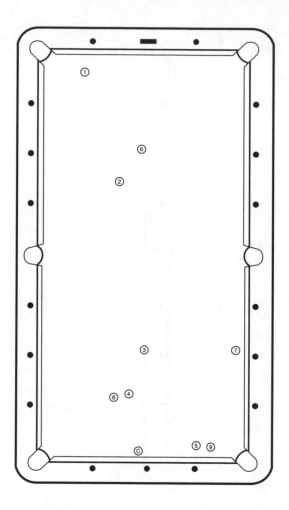

Diagram 109.

Since the odds are greatly against your hitting the 1 here—the 4, 8, 3, 2, and 6 are all in your way—get that dead 5-9 combination off the table. The 9 will be respotted harmlessly behind the 3, so even though you surrender cue-ball-in-hand to your opponent, he's limited in what he can do with it. This is a very basic Nine-Ball defensive move.

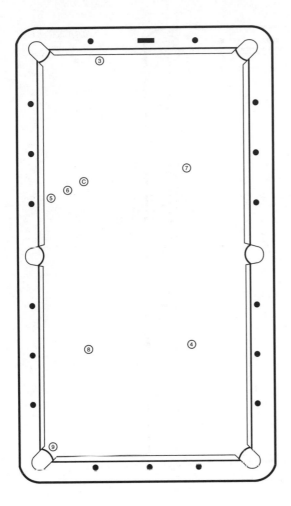

Diagram 110.

You could bank the 3-ball into the 9-ball for the win here—but if you miss, and leave the cue ball in the clear, you're very likely to lose outright. The smarter shot by far is to attempt a two-rail billiard off the 3 with the cue ball, using a thin hit and right-center English . . . especially since you have the chance to leave the 3 behind the 5 and the 6, and leave a safety with distance at the very least.

Point to remember: *When bank/combination shots come up, look for something else.*

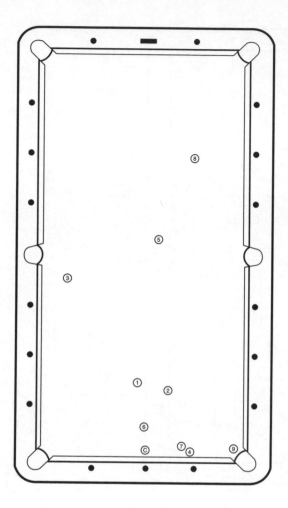

Diagram 111.

This time things aren't quite as cozy as they were in Diagram 109; you're hooked and the 9 cannot be protected, so you're going to have to kick (that is, send your cue ball to a rail first) to hit the 1. While we could easily do a section, and maybe a book, on the kick-shot variations of Nine-Ball, here are a few basic pointers: (a) The harder you shoot the cue ball into a rail at an angle, the shorter the angle at which it rebounds (especially on new cloth). (b) Your plan for how to hit the ball at which you're kicking should definitely include which side of the ball you want to hit—it sounds like splitting hairs, but it's critical. In this diagram, for instance, you just about *have* to contact the side of the 1 nearest you or risk losing the game straightaway. (c) When you shoot the cue ball into a rail at an angle and use English, one cue tip's worth of English will generally widen the rebound angle by close to one table diamond, so use spin judiciously when you kick.

In this diagram, shooting the cue ball right at the first diamond on the rail—with speed—should produce the result you want. It might look like you're aiming too high on the rail, but remember point (a) above. If you execute correctly, you might even slide over to the 2 and then to the 9 for the win.

Diagram 112.

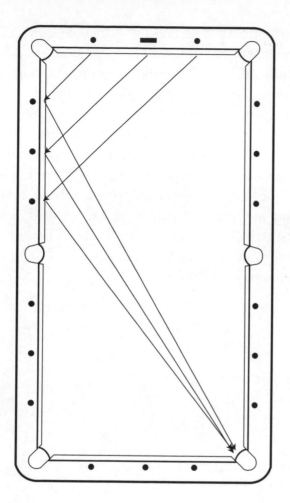

Here's a decent start on learning the game's diagonal angles. What you see here are natural ball paths from points on the end rail to cross the table diagonally and get to a corner pocket. When your cue ball and the object ball at which you're kicking lie along these lines, now you know where to aim, or compensate accord-ingly. When they're not along these precise lines, lines parallel to these will work, too. And when other balls interfere with these paths, you still have English available to change the path. These paths should also help with your cross-corner bank shots.

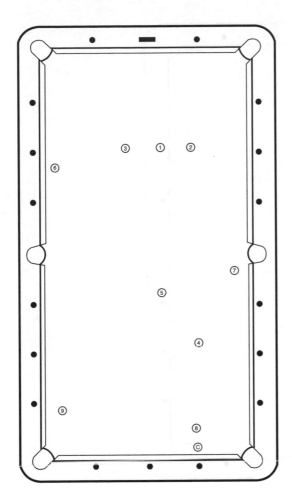

Diagram 113.

Combining what you've learned in the last two diagrams, you can now see that to hit the 1 here you'd aim at the third diamond up on the long rail. If you instead needed to hit the 2, you'd aim at a point about halfway between the second and third diamonds. And if you were after the 3, you'd use the third diamond again, this time adding one cue tip's worth of right-hand English.

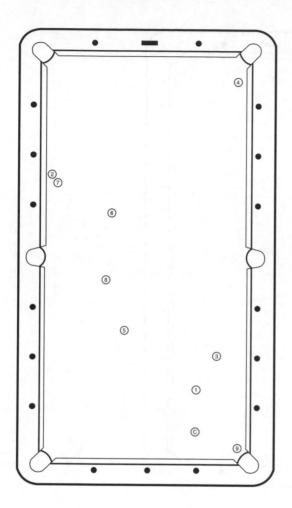

Diagram 114.

Banking the 1-ball into the 9-ball will work, but just barely; it's a high-risk shot. The cue ball is far enough off the rail here to try the billiard off the 1 instead, and inside, or left-hand, draw (about 7 o'clock on the cue ball) will help you bring the cue ball straight back to the 9 (right-hand or center draw might make the cue ball slide over too far to help you). More conservative players would bank the 1 behind the 2 and the 7 and try to hide the cue ball behind the 3. The most conservative players of all will pocket the 9, simply because of the nonnegotiable 2-7 combination—especially if the cue ball is close to or on that end rail.

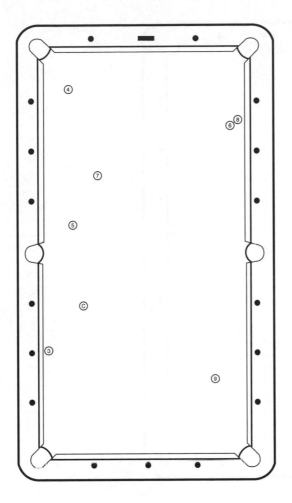

Diagram 115.

Nine-Ball will probably ask you to cut a ball thin along a rail more often than any other form of pool. You simply must have this shot in your arsenal, and you should develop your skill to include cutting the ball either to your left or right, with all different types of cue-ball action. Your comfort level with this family of shots ought to be such that you use the 3 here to send your cue ball back to deal with the unruly 6-8 combination with low right English, especially with the 4 close at hand across the way.

Diagram 116.

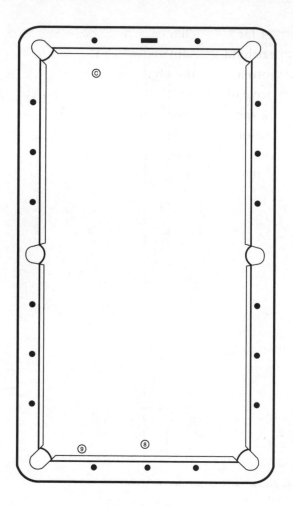

Your opponent might be thrilled with this safety he's left you, but actually your options are more fertile here than they might appear. You can return the safety by cutting the 8 thin on the side away from the 9, if you're accurate enough; you can hit it full, crossing over it, to leave your opponent the same situation going the other way; you can try to bank it in either back corner pocket; and with the 8 that far off the rail, you can go in behind it and try to kick it back into a corner, perhaps the best move of all since it's so easy to stick the cue ball right there for position on the 9 should the 8 go in. When the game offers you the chance to leave your opponent something like this, try to leave the object ball a bit farther over, with no bank-shot opportunities (and, naturally, closer to the end rail if possible). That leave would offer no easy safety, and one of the toughest cut shots in all pool.

Diagram 117.

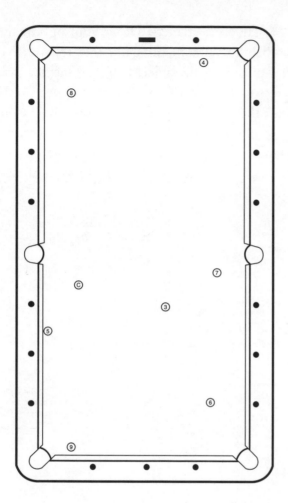

This illustrates the importance of missing on the professional side. If you can bank the 3 cross-corner, you've got natural position on the 4 and the game is probably yours—but you don't dare leave a 3-9 combination. So if you don't score here, you must bring the 3 in on the long-rail side. Then, assuming your shot was close enough, it should drop down on the wrong side of the 9 for a good safety.

Diagram 118.

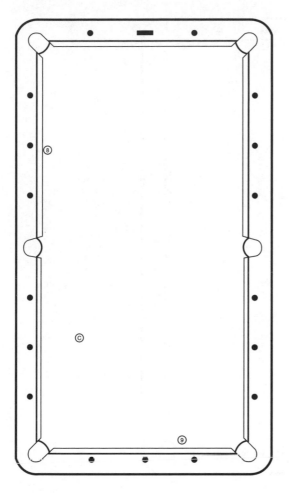

How do you propose to get position here? If you draw the cue ball, you risk a scratch in the opposite side pocket or insufficient angle on the 9-ball. If you use follow, your cue-ball route off that frozen 8-ball will be highly unpredictable and may not have enough speed anyway. The right way to play this is to really dig in to your cue ball with extreme 5 o'clock English, hit it hard, and *be sure to hit the rail just in front of the 8*. Correctly struck, the cue ball should travel almost straight across the table, showing more sidespin than topspin (you can tell by the speed), then take a humongous angle of rebound off that opposite long rail to bring you back down where you want to be. This is advanced, and tough, but once again, the situation recurs frequently in Nine-Ball. You need this shot in your game.

Diagram 119.

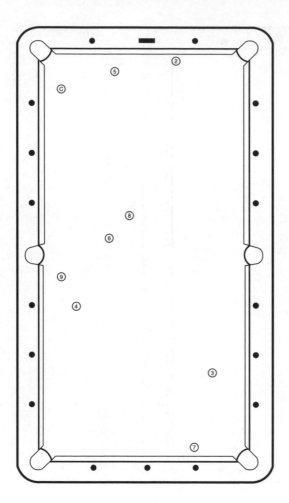

Two points about your kick at the 2-ball here: (a) You'll need to use English (high left) to create a productive angle off the opposite long rail, and (b) you need to hit the rail in front of the 2. That will give you your best chance either to pocket the 2, or to bring the cue ball away for a safety with distance if you don't.

Diagram 120.

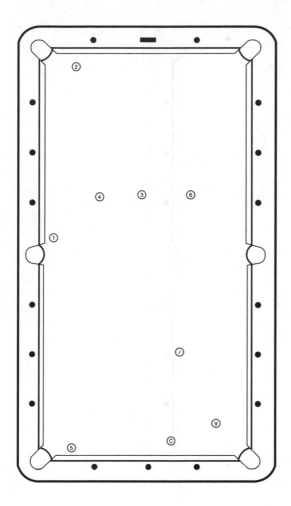

Obviously, you can't shoot the 1 in the corner. It's not a terribly tough kick into the side off the far end rail, but your position on the 2 will be uncertain. Consider shooting straight into the 1, driving it around the table and back down to the other end, while your cue ball follows toward the end rail. The 4, 3, and 6 cover far more ground than you might think as sentries out there, and you're quite likely to leave your opponent hooked. Opportunities like this frequently come up early in a Nine-Ball rack. Watch for them.

A FEW FINAL THOUGHTS

There are not nearly enough trees in this galaxy to provide the paper required to publish all the pool layouts you will ever see. Accordingly, one of my fonder hopes, as I said in the first pages, is that you won't wait for layouts highly similar or identical to those you've seen here to begin applying the concepts you've learned. Pool being as infinite as it is, there is no way to quantify or rank the importance of the points you've been shown for the various games, nor is there any way of knowing whether they are indeed the 40 most critical points to be taught in each type of game.

What I can tell you for sure is that they are not only highly significant, but highly extendable. Best of all, once you've fallen into the habit of thinking the game of pool through correctly, these concepts will help lead you to some realizations you can make on your own.

At that point, you should be beating the pants off just about everyone you know. I wish you that. And please refer your victims to me.